THE
COMPLETE
CAT
BREED
BOOK

DK

THE
COMPLETE
CAT
BREED
BOOK

Consultant Editor
DR. KIM DENNIS-BRYAN

DK LONDON

Senior Editors Gill Pitts, Paula Regan
Project Art Editor Laura Roberts-Jensen
Additional Design Tannishtha Chakraborty, Amy Orsborne
Editors Lizzie Munsey, Steve Setford
Editorial Assistant Alexandra Beeden
US Senior Editors Lori Hand, Rebecca Warren
US Editors Kayla Dugger, Kate Johnsen
Jacket Design Development Manager Sophia MTT
DK Picture Library Claire Bowers, Martin Copeland, Claire Cordier,
Emma Shepherd, Romaine Werblow
Senior Picture Researcher Myriam Megharbi
Commissioned Photography Tracy Morgan
Database Rob Laidler, David Roberts
Production Editor Kavita Varma
Production Controller Laura Andrews
Managing Editors Angeles Gavira Guerrero, Esther Ripley
Managing Art Editor Michael Duffy
Publisher Laura Buller
Art Director Karen Self
Design Director Phil Ormerod
Associate Publishing Director Liz Wheeler
Publishing Director Jonathan Metcalf

Consultant Editor Kim Dennis-Bryan
Contributors Ann Baggaley, Jolyon Goddard, Wendy Horobin

DK INDIA

Managing Editors Pakshalika Jayaprakash, Rohan Sinha
Senior Editor Sreshtha Bhattacharya
Editors Nandini Gupta, Antara Moitra, Priyanjali Narain
Assistant Editor Archana Ramachandran
Managing Art Editors Sudakshina Basu, Romi Chakraborty
Senior Art Editors Govind Mittal, Vaibhav Rastogi
Art Editors Mahipal Singh, Amit Varma
Assistant Art Editors Tanvi Nathyal, Tanvi Sahu
Design Consultant Shefali Upadhyay
Senior Jacket Designer Suhita Dharamjit
Jacket Designer Tanya Mehrotra
Picture Research Manager Taiyaba Khatoon
Picture Researcher Sakshi Saluja
DTP Designers Vishal Bhatia, Rakesh Kumar, Sachin Singh,
Mohammad Usman, Anita Yadav
Pre-production Manager Balwant Singh
Production Manager Pankaj Sharma
Editorial Head Glenda R. Fernandes
Design Head Malavika Talukder

For the curious
www.dk.com

CONTENTS

1 INTRODUCTION TO CATS

INTRODUCTION TO CATS

WHAT IS A CAT?

The domestic cat is now the world's most popular pet, but cats were not always tame. The relationship between humans and cats began in the Near East about 10,000 years ago, when cats killed the rodents that ate grain stored in towns and villages. They were kept as pets in Egypt from about 2000 BCE, but the different breeds have only been created over the last hundred years or so.

Cats are fast-moving natural athletes

Evolution of the cat

The family history of the domestic cat goes way back in time, to long before the first humanlike primates walked the Earth. All cats—from tigers, jaguars, and other big cats to smaller lynxes and ocelots—belong to the family of mammals called Felidae, which contains 48 living species. The first catlike carnivores appeared around 35 million years ago. Fossil evidence suggests that modern felids arose in Asia about 11 million years ago. However, the big cats we know today, such as the lion, did not evolve until much later, between 4 and 2 million years ago, when a drier, warmer climate gave rise to open habitats and herds of soft-skinned grazing animals. The athletic build of big cats was ideal for catching such prey. Less agile cats, such as the sabre-tooths, gradually died out.

The most recent cats to evolve include the lynxes (US and Europe), the bobcat (US), the leopard cat (Southeast Asia), and the wildcats (Africa, Europe, and Asia). The domestic cat is descended from the African wildcat, and it is now considered a species in its own right—*Felis catus*.

Domestication

In the Near East, about 10,000 years ago, humans began growing cereal crops and storing grain for the first time. They found that rats and mice would get into their stores and eat the grain. However, the rodents themselves were eaten by small predators, such as the African wildcat. Soon a relationship between cats and humans developed: the cats had a ready supply of food in the rodents that

---

THE CAT FAMILY

■ **This diagram** shows the relationship between the domestic cat and some of the other members of the cat family—the Felidae—based on genetic evidence. The closer a cat is to the domestic cat on this diagram, the more similar their genetic makeup.

■ **All Felidae** are carnivores—they eat exclusively meat and could not survive on a plant-based diet.

■ **Though they vary** in size, most cats share some physical characteristics—they have lithe, muscular bodies, large eyes, and retractable claws, and most have tails that measure up to half of their body length.

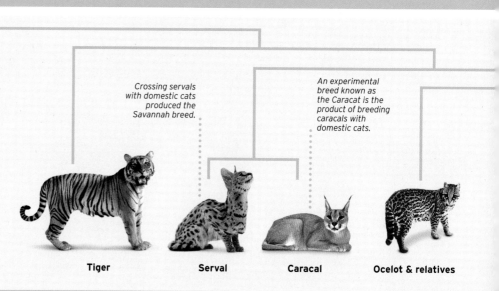

Crossing servals with domestic cats produced the Savannah breed.

An experimental breed known as the Caracat is the product of breeding caracals with domestic cats.

Tiger   **Serval**   **Caracal**   **Ocelot & relatives**

humans attracted, and the humans gained a much-appreciated form of pest control that lived alongside them in their towns and villages.

Wild species of cats are naturally wary of humans, but over time natural selection favored those cats that were least scared of people and adaptable enough to change from being solitary hunters to living in close proximity to humans and other cats. By around 2000 BCE the cat had become fully domesticated and was living in the homes of the Ancient Egyptians as a much-loved pet that also kept rodents under control. From Egypt the domestic cat would eventually spread to homes in nations around the world.

Cat breeds

In the late 19th century the breeding and showing of cats began in earnest, and cat enthusiasts became known as "cat fanciers." Cat registries were established to set breed standards and to store the genealogies of purebred cats. Today, there are several international cat registries, and more than 100 different cat breeds, though not all registries recognize the same ones. Breeds are defined by characteristics such as body and head shape; coat color and pattern; eye shape and color; and temperament; as well as by unusual features such as hairlessness, short tails, and folded ears.

Purebred cats have been selectively bred over many generations to perfect the desired characteristics of their breed. However, it is still possible for two cats in the same litter to be classed as different breeds, depending on which features they inherit from their parents.

WILD BEHAVIOR
Domestic cats display many of the same instincts as their wild relatives. For example, they stretch frequently, to keep their muscles limber in case they need to sprint after prey or away from danger.

Early cat breeds were often natural breeds, typical of certain regions of the world. These include the Maine Coon (from the state of Maine) and the Turkish Van (from Turkey). Today, breeders understand how traits are inherited and use cats with novel characteristics to produce new breeds—for example, with curled ears. New breeds can also result from crossing domestic cats with wild relatives, such as the Bengal (part leopard) and Savannah (part serval). Most pet cats are randomly bred "moggies," without any defined breed.

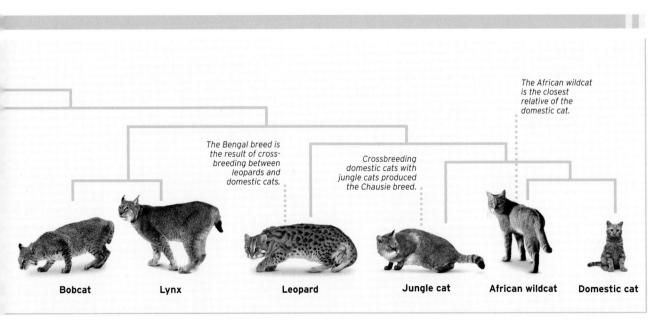

The African wildcat is the closest relative of the domestic cat.

The Bengal breed is the result of cross-breeding between leopards and domestic cats.

Crossbreeding domestic cats with jungle cats produced the Chausie breed.

Bobcat   Lynx   Leopard   Jungle cat   African wildcat   Domestic cat

The founder effect

Domestic cats spread around the world from Egypt, traveling with humans along trade routes on land and also aboard ships sailing to newly discovered lands, such as the Americas. These cats soon established isolated populations in new locations. If any of the pioneer cats in an area possessed an unusual trait, that characteristic stood a good chance of becoming common in future generations. In larger populations of mixed cats, these traits would usually disappear, especially if they caused disease or a disadvantage.

The genetic influence of these pioneering cats is known as the founder effect, and it explains why certain unusual traits still persist in some regions today. The best-known examples of the founder effect are the taillessness seen in the Manx cats of the Isle of Man and the polydactylism (a genetic mutation producing extra toes) that is common in cats along the East Coast of the US.

A CAT WITH MANY TOES
Cats with extra toes are called polydactyl cats. Polydactyl cats are common in breeds and populations along the East Coast.

trait to appear, the allele is recessive—the longhair allele is recessive as are some coat colours (see box below). If a cat has both a dominant shorthair allele and a recessive longhair allele, the recessive longhair allele is masked. The cat will be a shorthair—there is no intermediate effect (i.e., mid-length hair).

Sometimes genes mutate—their structure changes—and they produce a different trait. Some of these mutations can then be passed down to future generations. By using cats with desirable genetic mutations, breeders can create new breeds of cats—for example, with curly hair. However, many serious diseases are also caused by genetic mutation, and focusing on breeding within a very narrow gene pool to promote specific traits can result in the appearance of new diseases and disorders (pp.244-245).

COAT LENGTH AND GENETICS
The length of a cat's coat is controlled by a gene—the most common type produces a short coat. This is dominant over the type that creates a long coat, so if a cat has a copy of each it will be shorthaired.

Cat genetics

Genes carry all the information necessary for life. They control not only the chemical processes in a cat's body, but also the information that dictates the cat's physical characteristics, such as eye color and shape, coat color, and coat length. Genes are found on structures called chromosomes, which are located in the nuclei of body cells. Domestic cats have 38 chromosomes—two sets of 19 corresponding pairs. One set of chromosomes is inherited from the father, and the other set from the mother. Because of this, offspring inherit a mixture of their parents' characteristics. Each trait is determined by a specific piece of DNA, called a gene, which has two alleles—one from each parent.

If just one copy of an allele is needed for a trait to appear, it is referred to as dominant—for example, the allele for a tabby coat is dominant. If two copies of an allele are needed for a

DOMINANT AND RECESSIVE ALLELES

Cats with dark coats have at least one copy of the dominant allele "*D*", which produces hair packed with pigment. The recessive allele "*d*" of the pigment gene reduces the level of pigment, diluting the colour of a cat's fur. So, if two black-coated cats (with two copies of the black-coat allele "*B*", and one of each of the dense pigment alleles "*D*" and "*d*") were crossed with each other, there is a one-in-four chance of a kitten inheriting the recessive pigment allele from both parents. This would result in a kitten with blue (diluted black) fur coat.

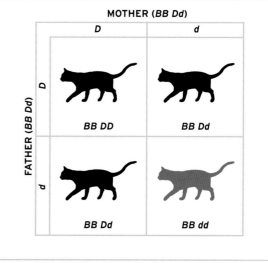

MOTHER (*BB Dd*)

	D	d
D	BB DD	BB Dd
d	BB Dd	BB dd

FATHER (*BB Dd*)

A CAT IN BLUE
A "blue" cat has two copies of the recessive dilute pigment allele. Cats inheriting two copies of the dominant dense pigment allele—or one of each kind of pigment allele—will have black fur.

Cat anatomy

The feline body-plan is that of a predator. The skeleton, which evolved for speed and agility, has slender limbs, a flexible spine, and a narrow ribcage to protect the heart and lungs, both of which are adapted for short bursts of speed. The shoulder blades are not attached to the rest of the skeleton but held in place by muscles and ligaments, allowing the cat to extend its stride when running.

A domestic cat's brain is about 25 percent smaller than that of a wildcat. This is because the areas of a wildcat's brain involved in mapping a large territory are no longer needed by domestic cats,

CAT'S WHISKERS
These are long, mobile sensory hairs that have been modified into touch sensors. They help with navigation in the dark and with detection of objects that are very close by.

EYES IN THE DARK
The large, wide-set eyes face forward for judging distances when hunting. Night vision is enhanced by the tapetum lucidum, a reflective layer behind the retina that bounces any light entering the eye back through the retina.

Ears can rotate independently to locate sources of sounds

Beneath the coat, the skin is usually the same color as the cat's fur

CARNIVORE TEETH
An adult cat has 30 teeth. The incisors are used for grasping and grooming, the canines for stabbing and gripping prey, and the carnassials (modified molars) at the side for cutting flesh.

A typical cat coat has an underlayer of soft, short hairs and mid-length insulating awn, overlaid by long, protective guard hairs

TOES AND CLAWS
Cats are digitigrade, which means that they walk on their toes. The toes have curved claws for scratching (which also sharpens them), fighting, and gripping. The claws are retractable: they can be slid back into sheaths for stealthy movement.

Front legs have greater range of movement than the hindlegs, allowing a cat to clean its head with its front paws

Paws have fleshy, hairless pads on their underside to provide support

which patrol much smaller ranges. Domestic cats are also a little smaller than their wild cousins.

Being carnivores, cats have a relatively short intestinal tract, because it is easier to digest meat than plant matter. A domestic cat's tract is a little longer than that of a wildcat. This reflects dietary changes—primarily the cereal content in food scraps scavenged from humans over millennia.

Cats have scent-producing glands in the skin around the mouth and tail, and also on the paws. They mark their territory using these scents and by scratching surfaces.

A cat's eyes are highly sensitive to small movements but their color vision is poor, since cats are primarily nocturnal animals. Cats have a wider range of hearing than humans, enabling them to detect the high-pitched squeaks of rodents. In addition to acute senses of taste and smell, cats have a sensory organ in the roof of the mouth—the vomeronasal, or Jacobson's, organ. To use this organ, cats contort their face (an action called the Flehmen response) as they pick up scents—usually those left by other cats. The several sets of whiskers on the face are highly sensitive to touch and air currents.

PREDATORY NATURE
Cats have evolved into superb hunters: they have sharp senses to detect their prey, a lithe, athletic body capable of bursts of speed to chase it down, and ferocious claws and teeth to catch and kill it.

RIGHTING REFLEX
When a cat falls from a fence or tree, it has the innate ability—and amazing flexibility—to twist its body right-side up. As soon as it senses disorientation, the cat rotates its head, followed by its front legs, and finally the hindquarters. The soft pads of the feet and flexible joints help absorb the shock of landing. A fall or drop, however, can still prove dangerous to a cat.

Head turns

Front legs come around

COMMON FEATURES OF A CAT
All domestic cats have a similar design. Selective breeding has produced some variations in body size and shape, but almost all breeds are still recognizably close relatives of their wildcat ancestors.

A cat uses the position and movement of its tail to signal its mood

Hindquarters rotate

Powerful hindlegs propel a cat when running and pouncing

Legs are a little shorter than those of a wildcat

CAT BALANCING
The tail aids balance. Its highly complex range of muscles gives it a wide range of movement.

Legs extend for landing

Body shapes

Eastern breeds, such as the Siamese, tend to have a slender and supple body with thin limbs and tail. This shape particularly suits a warm climate because it gives the body a large surface area, in relation to its volume, from which excess heat can disperse. Western breeds, such as the British Shorthair and most longhairs, are suited to temperate and cool regions. They tend to have a thickset, or cobby, body with a stockier tail and limbs. In this instance, the shape minimizes the body's surface area and helps to reduce heat loss. Other breeds such as the Ragdoll, have a body shape somewhere between these two extremes.

Slender athletic body

Intermediate body

Cobby body

Head shapes

There are three basic head shapes found in cat breeds. Most cats, including the British, European, and American Shorthairs, resemble their wildcat relatives, having a round head with a wedge-shaped face. In certain breeds, including the Siamese and the Devon Rex, the face has a much more elongated, or extreme, wedge shape. Other breeds, such as the Persian, are described as doll-faced. In these breeds the cat's face is round with a flat nose, which sometimes causes breathing difficulties.

Rounded wedge face

Long wedge face

Rounded flat face (front)

Rounded flat face (side)

Tails

Most domestic cats have a long tail, although it is slightly shorter than that of their wild ancestors. The tail is used for balance and communication. In Eastern breeds the tail is often thin with an elastic quality described as whippy. The defining characteristic of breeds such as the American and Japanese Bobtails and the Manx, however, is a short, stumpy tail—sometimes curved or kinked—or even a total absence of one. Another breed, the American Ringtail, has an unusual-looking curl in its tail; this is due to the cat's stronger-than-normal tail muscles, rather than any skeletal deformity.

Long tail

Bob tail

Ring tail

Eye color and shape

Domestic cats have large, alluring eyes that come in a wide variety of orange, green, and blue tones. Some cats even have odd-colored eyes, usually with one blue eye and one green or orange. Eye shapes can vary too, according to the breed of cat. Some breeds—for example, the Chartreux and the Persian—have round eyes, while others, such as the Maine Coon, retain the slightly slanted eyes of their wild ancestors. In some breeds of Oriental cat, including the Siamese, the slant of the eyes is even more pronounced, producing an almondlike shape.

Almond-shaped and blue

Slanted and green

Round and gold

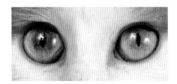

Round and odd-colored

Ear shapes

Almost all cat breeds have large, erect ears shaped like a half-cone, similar to those of their wildcat ancestors. In some breeds, such as the Siamese and Angora, the ear tips are pointed. Hair tufts at the tips, as in the Maine Coon, further accentuate the ears, so that they resemble those of a lynx. Other breeds, such as the British Shorthair and Abyssinian, have round-tipped ears. Two breeds have highly unusual ears caused by genetic mutations: the American Curl has ears that curl backward away from its face toward the rear of the skull; in the Scottish Fold, a fold in the ear cartilage bends the ears down toward the front of the head.

Pointed tips

Rounded tips

Curled

Folded

Coat types

Coats are generally made up of three types of hair: down, awn, and guard. Soft, wavy down and fine, mid-length awn form an insulating undercoat, while the longer, stiffer guard hairs form a protective outer coat. The lengths and proportions of these types of hair vary among breeds, and not all breeds have all three types. Most cats are shorthaired, like their wild ancestors. Long hair is caused by a recessive allele. In Persians the hair may reach up to 5in (12cm) long. Curly, or rexed, coats are caused by genetic mutations; there are now several rexed breeds, including the Cornish Rex and American Wirehair. There are also breeds, such as the Sphynx, with mutations that cause hairlessness.

Hairless

Short-coated

Curly coated

Long-coated

COAT COLORS AND PATTERNS

Cats come in a bewildering range of colors and coat patterns—there are endless combinations. Some breeds are defined specifically for their color, such as the blue-only Chartreux, and others for just one kind of coat pattern, such as the pointed Siamese. In many other breeds any combination of color and pattern is acceptable.

Coat color is produced by two forms of the pigment melanin: eumelanin (black and brown) and pheomelanin (red, orange, and yellow). Except for white hair, all colors—in solid and diluted forms—are derived from the varying amounts of these two pigments in the shafts of a cat's hair.

A cat's ancestral coat pattern is tabby. Selective breeding, however, has also created a wide range of other coat types, mostly produced by the expression of recessive alleles. Popular patterns include solid-color, coats, pointed coats, smoke coats, and coats that have a mixture of colors, as seen in torties and bicolors.

White hair lacks pigment, and the white allele (W) is dominant over all other color-producing alleles and coat patterns. Therefore, cats with colored and patterned coats have two recessive forms of the white allele (ww). Solid white is considered a Western color (see below).

White coat

Western colors
Coat colors traditionally found in European and American cats, such as British Shorthairs, Maine Coons, and Norwegian Forest Cats, are known as Western colors. Specifically, they are black and red, along with their respective diluted forms, blue and cream. Bicolored (a mixture of white patches and one of the Western colors) and solid-white coats are often described as Western too. Today, Western colors have a global presence, having been successfully introduced into Oriental cats. Burmese cats, for example, are often bred so that their coats bear Western reds and creams.

Black

Red

Blue

Cream

Eastern colors
Chocolate and cinnamon—and their respective diluted forms, lilac and fawn—are traditionally considered Eastern colors. These colors are thought to have originated in breeds such as the Siamese and the Persian. Nowadays, however, this separation of Eastern and Western colors is somewhat blurred, with cat colors having been transposed through breeding from one group of breeds to the other. All but the most conservative cat registries today accept Eastern colors in Western breeds, and vice versa. British Shorthairs, for example, are accepted in Eastern colors.

Chocolate

Cinnamon

Lilac

Fawn

UNDERSTANDING COAT COLORS

Pigmentation in cat fur varies from an even distribution along the hair shaft, which produces a solid-color coat, to no pigment at all, which produces white fur. A solid coat's color is determined by the density of the pigment in its hairs. Diluted red, for example, becomes cream. If just the end of each hair has color, the coat is tipped, shaded, or smoke, depending on exactly how much of the shaft holds color. Ticked shafts with alternating dark and light bands give a tabby color called agouti.

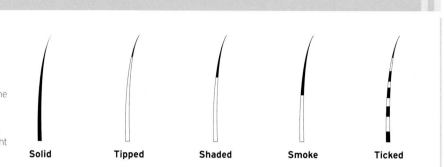

| Solid | Tipped | Shaded | Smoke | Ticked |

Tipped fur

When just the very tip of each cat hair—about one-eighth of the overall length—is strongly pigmented, the effect is known as tipped, shell, or chinchilla. The rest of the hair's length is usually white (unpigmented), although in some breeds yellow or reddish colors have also been produced. Tipping is controlled by the interaction of several different genes. Some Burmillas, Persian Chinchillas, and Persian Cameos have tipped coats.

Light chocolate tipped

Blue-tipped silver

Shaded fur

In shaded coats the upper quarter of each hair shaft has color. This pattern is produced by the same genes responsible for tipped fur but in shaded cats the coat appears darker on the back, where the fur lies flat. The heavier degree of tipping in shaded fur produces a dramatic rippling effect as the cat moves. Shaded coats are accepted and sought after in many breeds, especially Persians.

Cream shaded Cameo

Silver shaded

Smoke fur

About half of the hair shaft (the uppermost half) has color in smoke fur. When still, many smoke cats appear to have a solid coat with just a paler neck ruff, but when the cat moves, the lighter roots become more visible and the cat shimmers. Smokes are very popular and are found in many breeds, including the Manx, Exotic Shorthairs and Longhairs, Maine Coons, and Persians. Smoke kittens are often difficult to tell apart from solid kittens, since the smoke effect can take a few months to appear.

Black smoke

Blue smoke

Ticked fur

In ticked coats the hair shafts have alternating pigmented and paler bands (see box, above). The tips of the hair shafts are always pigmented. Ticked fur is a characteristic of many wild cats and other mammals, and it provides good camouflage. Ticked, or agouti, hair makes up the lighter areas of tabby coats. A full, unpatterned agouti coat is a characteristic of Abyssinians and their longhaired relatives, Somalis. Abyssinians have 4 to 6 bands of color on each hair and Somalis up to 20.

Silver sorrel

Ruddy

Particolors

Particolored cats, or partis, have two or more definite colors in their coats. Partis include bicolor and tricolor cats and are found in many breeds, both shorthair and longhair. Partis also include torties (see below), with white spotting. Even a small amount of white counts as particoloring. When tortoiseshells have a high proportion of white fur, the pattern is described as calico, or tortie and white. Particolored cats are almost always female.

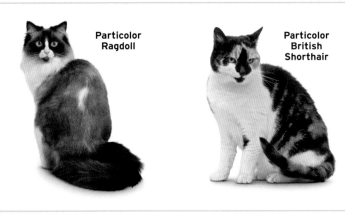

Particolor Ragdoll

Particolor British Shorthair

Tortie colors

Torties, or tortoiseshells, have distinct or mingled patches of black (or chocolate or cinnamon) and red fur. Variations include the diluted forms of these colors: blue, lilac, fawn, and cream. The pattern usually only occurs in females; on rare occasions the pattern may occur in a male, possibly due to a chromosomal abnormality. Torties with tabby markings are known as patched tabbies, and these cats are classed as particolors (see above).

Oriental Tortie

Asian Tortie

Pointed

Cats with dark extremities and pale body fur are described as pointed. In Siamese and Persian Colorpoints this recessive characteristic is controlled by a heat-sensitive enzyme involved in producing hair pigment. The enzyme works only in the cooler extremities of a cat's body— hence the darker fur on the face, ears, paws, and tail. Other pointed patterns—such as the Van, in which color is restricted to the ears and tail—are a form of white spotting (see below).

Solid-pointed Siamese

Turkish Van

White spotting

The allele responsible for white spotting on a cat's coat is dominant. It works by suppressing areas of colored fur to produce a coat that is bicolored or tricolored. The effect can range from almost totally white cats and the Van pattern (see above), to cats with just one or a few white patches in which the white fur is limited to the face, throat (bib), belly, and paws (mittens).

Non-pedigree shorthair with white bib and mittens

White-spotted Maine Coon

Tabby colors

The ancestral pattern consists of swirls, stripes, or spots of solid fur—commonly black, brown, red (ginger), or silver (gray)—mixed with paler areas of ticked, or agouti, fur. It acts as natural camouflage for a cat—a definite advantage when hunting for food in the wild. The tabby pattern is a dominant characteristic and its various forms are still common not only in old breeds, such as the Maine Coon, but also in newer wild-looking hybrids, such as the Savannah. The Classic Tabby has a blotched or swirling pattern; the Mackerel Tabby has stripes, like a fishbone, running down its sides; and the Spotted Tabby has spots or rosettes. Tabbies have fine lines on their head (usually an "M"-shaped mark on the forehead) and barring on their tail and legs.

Spotted **Ticked**

Classic **Mackerel**

HOW TO USE THE BREED CATALOG

Catalog entries will help you choose which cat is right for you. They outline the main features, appearance, and temperament of each breed, and specify any relevant care tips. At-a-glance data panels detail the origins, weight, and the breed registries that recognize the cat, along with the range of coat colors and patterns and the required grooming regime.

BREED REGISTRIES

Abbreviations indicate which of the world's four major breed registries recognize this particular type of cat.

CFA The Cat Fanciers' Association, Inc.

FIFe Fédération Internationale Féline

GCCF The Governing Council of the Cat Fancy

TICA The International Cat Association

GROOMING KEY

The comb symbol and blue bar indicate how frequently you will need to groom this breed of cat in order to maintain its coat in top condition.

Weekly

2–3 times a week

Daily

38 CATALOG OF BREEDS

SINGAPURA

THIS SMALLEST OF CAT BREEDS HAS A KITTENISH TEMPERAMENT

Place of origin	Singapore
Date of origin	1970s
Breed registries	CFA, FIFe, GCCF, TICA
Weight range	4–9lb (2–4kg)
Grooming	

Colors and patterns
Sepia agouti: seal brown ticking on ivory ground color.

The distinctive ticked coat of this little cat caught the eye of an American scientist, Hal Meadow, while he was working in Singapore in the 1970s. Meadow and his wife started a breeding program for the Singapura, which they carried out both in Singapore and the US. By the 1990s British breeders were also taking an interest in this cat. Singapuras are now known worldwide, although they are still very rare. Small in size but big in personality, these cats are prying and mischievous, happiest when exploring the world at a high level from a shelf or an owner's shoulder.

Dark facial markings on cheekbones

Long, strongly muscled legs

Sepia agouti coat paler on chin, chest, and underbelly

Large, deeply cupped ears

Enormous almond-shaped green eyes, set wide apart

Each hair of its fine, silky coat has alternate light and dark banding

Medium-long, slender tail has dark seal-brown tip

Firm, muscular body

Darker barring on inner forelegs and hind legs

CHOOSING THE RIGHT CAT

Cats make rewarding, lovable pets, but owning one can require a lot of time and money. If you think you would like to own a cat, you will need to do some research to make sure you are ready for the responsibility. If your heart is set on owning a purebred cat, you will need to make sure you find a reputable breeder, though you may also be able to find a purebred in a rescue center.

A pet cat can live for up to 20 years

Are you ready to own a cat?

Owning a cat might seem like a good idea, but you should give the idea serious consideration before you buy or adopt one. Consider if a cat will fit into your lifestyle. It is unfair to a cat to be left alone for long periods; they may seem independent, but cats need human companionship. Neglected outdoor cats may wander off, while indoor cats can become bored and destructive. It is not a good idea to get a cat if anyone in your household is allergic to cats or becomes asthmatic around them. Think carefully too if you have young children since you will need to spend time teaching them how to handle a cat.

Cats also mean changes to your home; you'll need to be able to cope with furnishings covered with cat hair and the occasional half-eaten bird or mouse. You will also need to cat-proof your house, keep breakable items out of reach, and remove potential hazards such as houseplants that can be poisonous to cats (p.203). You will need to find somewhere to put your cat's litter box, and get used to changing it regularly.

THE BEST BREED FOR YOU
Cat breeds come in many different sizes, coat types, and personalities. Do your research and work out which breeds will best suit your lifestyle—longhaired cats such as Persians (above) make beautiful companions but require a lot of grooming.

Cats can be expensive, and you need to make sure you can afford to cover the costs. There will be an initial outlay for your kitten or cat, which can reach hundreds of dollars for a purebred. Advances in veterinary medicine and better understanding of a cat's diet mean that cats now live longer than they used to, even for as long as 20 years. The cost of owning a cat can add up to thousands of dollars over the course of its life. Pet insurance will help cover some veterinary costs, but probably not vaccinations, neutering, or dental treatment. You will also need to buy food, bedding, cat litter, and other accessories on a regular basis. If you go away, you will need to pay for your cat to stay in a boarding kennel, or for someone to look after him at your home.

Deciding on a breed

If you would like a purebred cat, make sure you do your research, so that you know about the breed's needs and characteristics. If you are unsure which breed to choose, you might want to consider size, coat type, and temperament. Breeds vary in size, between about 9–20 lb (5–9 kg). Big cats are unlikely to take kindly to an indoor life in a small apartment. If you want a longhaired breed, you will have to groom your cat every day, otherwise its fur will become matted; shorthaired cats generally need much less grooming (pp.228-31). Temperaments vary between breeds—Asian cats such as the Siamese and Ocicat tend to be active and vocal, while heavier-set breeds such as the British Shorthair and Persian are usually quieter and more laid back.

You should also think about what gender and age of cat will suit you. Male cats are usually bigger than females and may be more outgoing, but both make trouble-free pets once neutered. If you're worried about housetraining a kitten, you could buy or rescue an adult cat. Finally, if there are stretches of the day when no one is at home, you might want to consider getting two cats, so that they can keep each other company.

NEW FAMILY MEMBER
Do plenty of research before you buy a cat or kitten, especially if you've never owned one before. A cat or kitten is a wonderful addition to the family, but can mean big changes in your routine.

Finding a breeder

Once you have decided which kind of cat breed you want, the best place to buy a purebred cat is from a reputable breeder. You can find cats in newspapers, online, or in store windows, but generally these vendors should be avoided because they are not usually cat experts. It is also inadvisable to buy a kitten from a pet store, since you will not be sure where the kittens have come from. Your local vet may be able to recommend a breeder to you, or you could find breeders from a cat club list, breed registry list, or at a cat show—many of the people who show cats also breed them or will be able to recommend a breeder.

At the breeders, make sure you ask lots of questions, so that you know you will get a healthy, well-adjusted cat (see right). The breeder should also ask you questions, to make sure that you are responsible enough to own a cat and can afford to look after it. You should research the going rate for kittens of the breed you would like. A higher cost can sometimes reflect top quality and better care and attention

10 IMPORTANT QUESTIONS TO ASK A BREEDER

- How long have you been breeding cats?
- Can I have references from your vet and previous customers?
- What are the important characteristics of this breed—will the kitten be "show quality" or "pet quality"?
- Does this breed suffer from any inherited diseases, and has the kitten been screened for them?
- How much time will I need to spend grooming?
- Has the kitten been socialized—will it be OK to introduce him to children and other pets?
- Will the kitten have been vaccinated and wormed by the time he's ready to be picked up?
- Have you registered the kitten with a registry, and may I have the printed pedigree?
- Can I have a written contract of sale, outlining both my and your (the breeder's) rights and responsibilities, and including an agreement that the purchase is subject to a vet's examination to check the kitten's health?
- Will I be able to contact you if I need advice after I bring the kitten home?

MEETING THE FAMILY
Kittens that have been socialized from an early age should not be timid or aggressive when encountering new people.

put in by the breeder. Some breeders offer "pet quality" as well as "show quality" kittens. Pet quality cats are just as healthy as show cats but have minor physical defects for the breed standard, and should be considerably cheaper than show quality cats. The breeder may ask you to sign an agreement not to enter pet quality cats in shows or to breed from them in order to keep breeding lines "pure."

It is important to meet the litter of kittens before you decide to buy one of them. A good breeder will let you observe the kittens and how they interact with their littermates. You should also meet the mother and check her health. She will give you an indication of your kitten's adult size, appearance, and temperament. The breeder may also own the father—if so, ask to see him too. The breeder can also give you an idea of the life span of the particular breed.

The kitten you choose to take home with you should appear healthy and alert, with a good muscle tone and a clean coat free from pests such as fleas. His eyes should be bright, there should be no discharge from the eyes or nose, the ears should be free of wax, and the gums should be pink. Make sure your kitten has been (or will be) vaccinated, wormed, and screened for any genetic disorders that are known to occur in the breed. Take any certificates for these home with you if or when you buy a kitten. Avoid buying a kitten if it appears ill, if it has been kept in isolation away from the rest of its litter, if you think the kittens are being reared in substandard conditions, or if the breeder doesn't seem to know

A CAT WITH HISTORY
Many different types of cats end up in shelters. If you decide to give a home to a cat that is elderly or disabled, the rescue center will sometimes help you to pay for its ongoing health care.

much about the breed or cat health care. If you're not happy, you can visit another breeder. If all goes well, you should pick up your inoculated, housetrained, and socialized kitten when it is about 12 weeks old.

Rescue centers

If you would like to give a home to a purebred cat, one place you may not have thought of looking is in a rescue center, or shelter, for cats. Usually run on a nonprofit basis, rescue centers are staffed mostly by volunteers and funded by private donations and adoption fees. They take in stray, unwanted, and feral cats and try to find suitable homes for them.

Purebred cats can show up in rescue centers from time to time. Generally, these will be the more common breeds such as the Siamese, Maine Coon, or Persian—you are less likely to find an unusual breed.

After visiting a rescue center and meeting all the cats waiting for homes, you may decide to adopt a mixed breed rather than a purebred cat. More than 95 percent of all domestic cats are mixed breed, and there are a large number of them housed in rescue shelters, each deserving of a loving home. Cat rescue centers are definitely worth investigating, especially if your preference is for a fully trained adult cat with an established personality.

If you decide to adopt from a rescue shelter, a member of staff will visit your home to check that it's safe and suitable for a cat, and to make sure that you will make a good cat owner. You will be charged an adoption fee, which helps cover vet costs for rescue cats' health care, such as inoculations, blood tests, neutering, and microchipping.

RESCUE CATS
The staff at a rescue center will assess the character of each cat and can help match you with your perfect pet; you may even find a purebred cat in need of a home.

CATALOG OF BREEDS

SNOW BENGAL
Bengal cats are the result of crossbreeding between domestic cats and the Asian leopard cat. This snow Bengal also has some albinistic genes, which accounts for its pale coloring.

SHORTHAIRS

Most cats have short hair, whether they are large or small, wild or domestic. This is an evolutionary development that makes sense for a natural predator relying on stealth and the occasional burst of speed. A hunting cat is more efficient in a short coat because it can glide unhampered through dense terrain and move freely for a rapid pounce in a tight corner.

A short coat keeps a cat warm without overheating

Developing the shorthair

The first cats to be domesticated, possibly over 4,000 years ago, had short hair, and their sleek-coated look has been popular ever since. In a short coat, colors and patterns are clearly defined and the feline form appears to full advantage. Dozens of shorthaired breeds have been developed, but there are three main groups: British, American, and Oriental Shorthairs. The first two are essentially ordinary domestic cats refined by decades of breeding programs. They are sturdy, round-headed cats, with short, dense, double-layered coats. The strikingly different Oriental group have little to do with the East, being created in Europe through crosses with the Siamese. They have short, close-lying, fine coats with no woolly undercoat.

Other well-loved shorthaired cats include: the Burmese; the plush-furred Russian Blue, which has a very short undercoat that lifts the top guard hairs away from the body; and the Exotic Shorthair, which combines unmistakably Persian looks with a shorter, more manageable coat.

Short hair is taken to extremes in several hairless breeds, including the Sphynx and the Peterbald. These cats are usually not totally hairless—most have a fine covering of body hair with the feel of suede. Another variety of short hair is seen in rexed cats, which have wavy or crimped coats. Among the best known of these are the Devon Rex and the Cornish Rex.

Easy maintenance

A great advantage for owners of shorthaired breeds is that the coat requires little grooming to keep it in good condition, while parasites and injuries are easy to see and treat. However, keeping a shorthaired cat does not guarantee hair-free carpets and sofas. Some breeds shed quite heavily, especially during seasonal loss of thick undercoats, and even single-coated varieties such as the Orientals always lose a certain amount of hair.

ASIAN SOLID
The Asian group of shorthairs are moderate in build, being neither stocky nor as ultra slim as the Orientals.

SIAMESE
The short, fine coat of the Siamese accentuates the elegant lines of this graceful, blue-eyed cat. Many different point colors have been developed, but the classic seal point remains a favorite.

EXOTIC SHORTHAIR

A LOW-MAINTENANCE VERSION OF THE LONGHAIRED PERSIAN CAT

Place of origin	US
Date of origin	1960s
Breed registries	CFA, FIFe, GCCF, TICA
Weight range	8–15 lb (3.5–7 kg)

Grooming

Colors and patterns
Almost all colors and patterns.

The first Exotics were bred in the US in the 1960s, and by the 1980s, there was a popular British version as well. These cats were created through breeding programs that crossed the Persian (or Longhair) with shorthairs, including the Burmese (p.40), Abyssinian (p.83), British Shorthair (pp.68–77), and American Shorthair (p.61). Exotics combine the Persian's sweet, round-faced look and quiet temperament with a lush but short coat that requires minimal grooming. These gentle cats are happy as indoor pets and are always pleased to have someone around to play with or offer a lap.

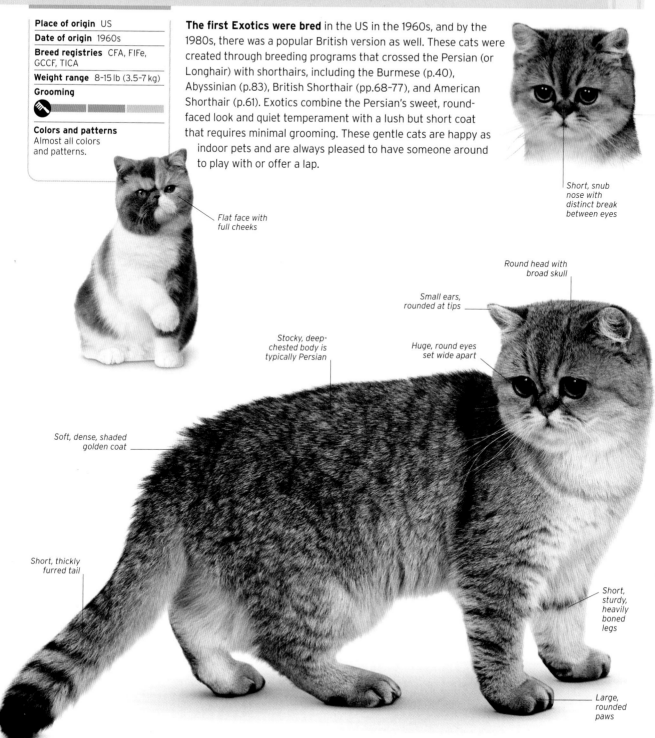

Short, snub nose with distinct break between eyes

Flat face with full cheeks

Round head with broad skull

Small ears, rounded at tips

Huge, round eyes set wide apart

Stocky, deep-chested body is typically Persian

Soft, dense, shaded golden coat

Short, thickly furred tail

Short, sturdy, heavily boned legs

Large, rounded paws

KHAOMANEE

AN EXTROVERTED AND INTELLIGENT BREED THAT IS EAGER TO DIVE INTO EVERYTHING

Place of origin Thailand

Date of origin 14th century

Breed registries CFA, GCCF, TICA

Weight range 6–12 lb (2.5–5.5 kg)

Grooming

Colors and patterns
White only.

The "white jewel," as the name translates, is a breed native to Thailand. Pure white cats, apparently of this type, are recorded in Thai history as early as the 14th century, but Khaomanees were not seen outside their native country until the late 20th century. Now they are attracting attention elsewhere, especially in the US and the UK. This aristocratic breed has a palette of eye colors: it may have eyes of the same color or of different colors, have eyes the same color but of varying shades, or even have eyes that are each bicolored. Khaomanees are bold, friendly, and sometimes loud-voiced.

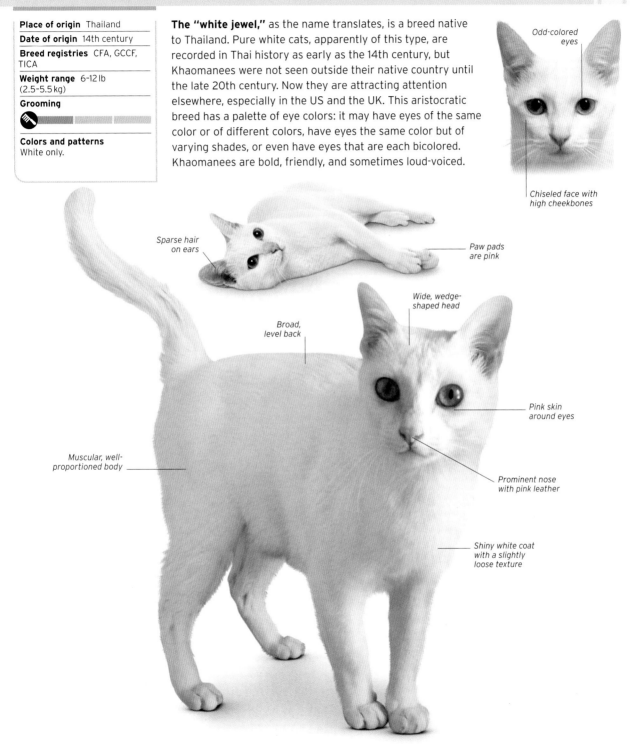

Odd-colored eyes

Chiseled face with high cheekbones

Sparse hair on ears

Paw pads are pink

Wide, wedge-shaped head

Broad, level back

Pink skin around eyes

Muscular, well-proportioned body

Prominent nose with pink leather

Shiny white coat with a slightly loose texture

KORAT

THIS ENCHANTING AND AFFECTIONATE CAT HAS A LONG AND PROUD HISTORY

Place of origin Thailand

Date of origin c.12th–16th century

Breed registries CFA, FIFe, GCCF, TICA

Weight range 6–10 lb (2.5–4.5 kg)

Grooming

Colors and patterns Blue only.

Few cat breeds can truly be described as being of ancient origin, but the Korat from Thailand is one of them. It appears in a book titled *The Cat Book Poems*, which dates back to the Ayudhya period (1350–1767), in what was then Siam. Long prized in its native country as a symbol of good fortune, the Korat was virtually unknown in the West until the mid-20th century, when a breeding pair was sent to the US. This graceful, silvery blue cat makes a very special pet. Usually highly active, the Korat has its peaceful moments, too, and is gentle and affectionate with its owners. With heightened senses, the breed is easily startled by loud noises or abrupt handling.

Large ears flare at base

Distinctive heart-shaped head

Oval paws

Lithe, muscular body

Very large, round green eyes

Close-lying, blue coat with no undercoat

Nose leather is heart shaped

Coat hairs are silver tipped

CHINESE LI HUA

A GOOD FAMILY CAT THAT NEEDS ROOM TO ROAM

Place of origin China

Date of origin 2000s

Breed registries CFA

Weight range 9–11 lb (4–5 kg)

Grooming

Colors and patterns
Brown mackerel tabby only.

Cats fitting the description of the Li Hua, or Dragon Li as it is also called, appear to have been common in China for centuries. However, around the world, this cat is a newcomer, recognized as an experimental breed only since 2003, although it is beginning to attract international interest. The Chinese Li Hua is a large cat with a muscular build and a beautifully marked tabby coat. Though not particularly demonstrative, it makes a friendly and faithful pet. This active cat, which has a reputation as a clever hunter, needs space to exercise and is not suited to a confined life in a small home.

Lower jaw slightly shorter than upper

Black spot at corner of mouth

Long, straight nose

Straight, muscular legs

Lighter hair on belly

Ticked hairs form mackerel pattern

Bright yellow eyes

Sturdy, rectangular body

Tail has ring marks and black tip

Unticked beige hairs on chin and chest

ASIAN–BURMILLA

AN ENCHANTING COMPANION CAT WITH DELIGHTFUL LOOKS AND TEMPERAMENT

Place of origin UK

Date of origin 1980s

Breed registries FIFe, GCCF, TICA

Weight range 9–15lb (4–7kg)

Grooming

Colors and patterns
Many shaded colors, including lilac, black, brown, blue, and tortoiseshell, with silver or golden ground color.

When the accidental mating of a lilac Burmese (p.39) with a Persian Chinchilla (p.140) in 1981 produced a litter of kittens with exceptionally beautiful coats, their owner was encouraged to experiment with further breeding. The result was the Burmilla, a cat of elegant Asian proportions, with large, appealing eyes and a delicately shaded or tipped coat; a longhaired version is also available. Although still uncommon, this charming and intelligent breed is becoming increasingly popular. It possesses a bit of the zany character of the Burmese, tempered by the quieter nature of the Chinchilla. The Burmilla enjoys games but also will settle on a lap for a peaceful snooze.

Large, expressive green eyes

Lilac shaded coat

Face and legs may have slight shading

Broad-based ears, slightly rounded at tips

Slight dip in nose

Graceful, elegantly proportioned body

Silky textured, close-lying coat

Medium-to-long, slightly tapered tail

Vestigial tabby markings

Silvery white ground color with chocolate tipping

Slender but strong legs

ASIAN–SMOKE

THIS PLAYFUL AND INTELLIGENT BREED IS VERY RESPONSIVE TO ATTENTION

Place of origin UK
Date of origin 1980s
Breed registries GCCF
Weight range 9–15lb (4–7kg)
Grooming

Colors and patterns
Any color topcoat,
  including tortoiseshell,
    with a silvery white
      undercoat.

Originally known as the Burmoire, this graceful cat is a cross between the Burmilla (opposite) and the Burmese (p.39). The Asian Smoke has one of the most attractive coats of all the Asian breeds: a deep, often solid color on top, the fur ripples apart when the cat moves or is stroked to reveal glimpses of a gleaming, silvery undercoat. An athletic, playful cat with an outgoing personality, the Asian Smoke is highly curious and loves to investigate everything. Asian Smokes are happy kept as indoor cats as long as they have plenty of human companionship, amusement, and affection.

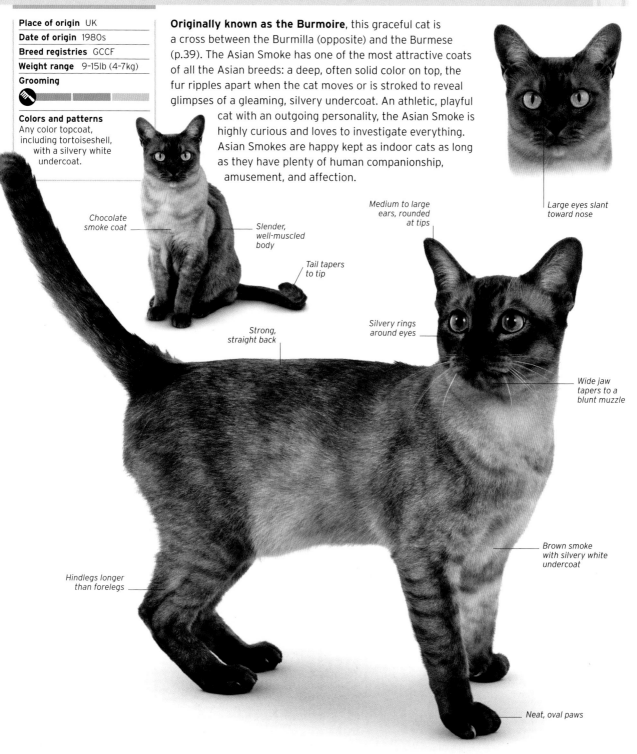

Large eyes slant toward nose

Chocolate smoke coat

Slender, well-muscled body

Tail tapers to tip

Medium to large ears, rounded at tips

Strong, straight back

Silvery rings around eyes

Wide jaw tapers to a blunt muzzle

Brown smoke with silvery white undercoat

Hindlegs longer than forelegs

Neat, oval paws

ASIAN–SOLID

LIVELY AND LOVING, THIS BREED IS VERY DEPENDENT ON COMPANY

Place of origin	UK
Date of origin	1980s
Breed registries	GCCF
Weight range	9–15lb (4–7kg)

Grooming

Colors and patterns
All solid colors and various tortoiseshells.

The result of experiments to create what is essentially a Burmese cat (p.39) with different coat colors, this British breed includes an all-black version known as the Bombay. The latter is easily confused with an American-bred black cat also called Bombay (p.36), which has a different breed history. The Asian Solid may be less inclined to be highly active in the household than its Burmese relative but can nevertheless make its presence known with an insistent voice when it wants attention, which is most of the time. This friendly, affectionate cat likes to follow its owner around with doglike devotion.

Obvious nose break

Kitten

Neat, oval paws

Medium to large ears with rounded tips

Golden eyes set wide apart

Medium-long tail carried gracefully

Straight back from shoulders to rump

Pink nose leather

Short, fine, close-lying red coat

Elegant, firmly muscled body

Hindlegs slightly longer than forelegs

ASIAN–TABBY

A SOCIABLE CAT THAT IS EASY TO KEEP IN A FAMILY HOME

Place of origin	UK
Date of origin	1980s
Breed registries	GCCF
Weight range	9–15lb (4–7kg)
Grooming	

Colors and patterns
Spotted, classic, mackerel, or ticked tabby patterns, in various colors.

This member of the Asian group of cats comes in four different tabby patterns: classic, mackerel, spotted, and ticked. The variety of stripes, swirls, rings, and spots occur in a wide range of beautiful colors. The most commonly seen pattern is the ticked tabby, in which each individual hair has contrasting bands of color. Like all its relations, the Asian Tabby has the graceful, muscular lines and extroverted personality of the Burmese cats (p.39) used in its development, blended with the quieter nature of the Persian Chinchilla (p.140). This breed makes a lovely family pet and is growing in popularity.

Amber eyes with Asian slant

Short, thick, glossy, brown mackerel tabby coat

Prominent cheekbones

Delicate, oval paws

Medium to large ears, set well apart

Blunt, wedge-shaped head

"M" marking on forehead

Straight-backed, muscular body

Rounded chest

BOMBAY

THIS PINT-SIZED "BLACK PANTHER" HAS GLOSSY FUR AND COPPERY EYES

Place of origin	US
Date of origin	1950s
Breed registries	CFA, TICA
Weight range	6–11lb (2.5–5kg)
Grooming	

Colors and patterns
Black only.

Created specifically for its appearance, the Bombay is a cross between the American Burmese (p.40) and the American Shorthair (p.61). Round and shiny, this breed comes only in black. It may look like a panther but it is a true homebody, and few cats are more loving and sociable. Bombays want to be with their owners all the time, and are likely to mope if left alone for too long. Having inherited the inquisitive and playful nature of the Burmese, these cats are no couch potatoes. Bombays enjoy a game and are ready to be entertained. They get along well with children and other pets.

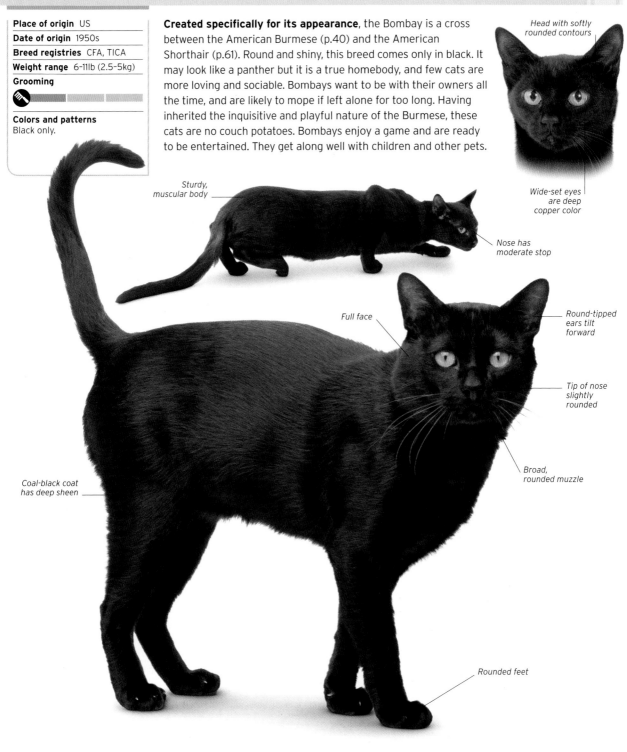

Head with softly rounded contours

Wide-set eyes are deep copper color

Sturdy, muscular body

Nose has moderate stop

Full face

Round-tipped ears tilt forward

Tip of nose slightly rounded

Broad, rounded muzzle

Coal-black coat has deep sheen

Rounded feet

NOT SHY
The lithe and gleaming Bombay is a cat that feels confident in company. This breed is prepared to make overtures to anyone who is likely to provide entertainment or a lap to sit on.

SINGAPURA

THIS SMALLEST OF CAT BREEDS HAS A KITTENISH TEMPERAMENT

Place of origin	Singapore
Date of origin	1970s
Breed registries	CFA, FiFe, GCCF, TICA
Weight range	4–9lb (2–4kg)

Grooming

Colors and patterns
Sepia agouti: seal brown ticking on ivory ground color.

The distinctive ticked coat of this little cat caught the eye of an American scientist, Hal Meadow, while he was working in Singapore in the 1970s. Meadow and his wife started a breeding program for the Singapura, which they carried out both in Singapore and the US. By the 1990s British breeders were also taking an interest in this cat. Singapuras are now known worldwide, although they are still very rare. Small in size but big in personality, these cats are prying and mischievous, happiest when exploring the world at a high level from a shelf or an owner's shoulder.

Dark facial markings on cheekbones

Long, strongly muscled legs

Sepia agouti coat paler on chin, chest, and underbelly

Large, deeply cupped ears

Enormous almond-shaped green eyes, set wide apart

Each hair of its fine, silky coat has alternate light and dark banding

Medium-long, slender tail has dark seal-brown tip

Firm, muscular body

Darker barring on inner forelegs and hind legs

EUROPEAN BURMESE

THIS CAT IS CONFIDENT, INQUISITIVE, AND FULL OF CHARACTER

Place of origin Burma (Myanmar)

Date of origin 1930s

Breed registries CFA, FIFe, GCCF, TICA

Weight range 8–14lb (3.5–6.5kg)

Grooming

Colors and patterns
Solid and tortoiseshell colors include blue, brown, cream, lilac, and red. Always in sepia pattern.

This breed was first developed in the US in the 1930s, using a foundation cat introduced from Southeast Asia. In the late 1940s several Burmese cats were sent from the US to the UK, where the breed acquired a different look. The European Burmese is slightly longer in the head and body than its American counterpart, and comes in a greater variety of colors. This sweet-natured cat has plenty of affection to offer and needs to be a full member of a loving family. A Burmese is not well suited to a home where it will be left to its own devices for long periods.

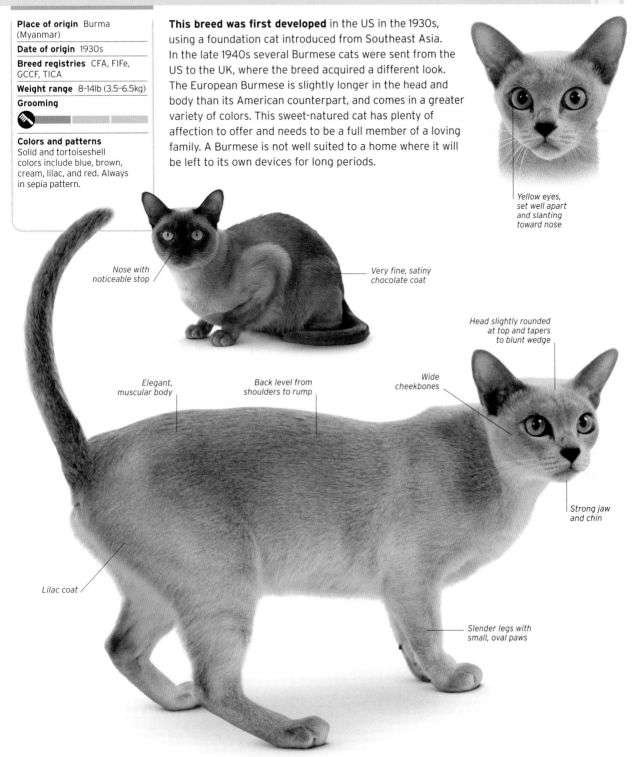

Yellow eyes, set well apart and slanting toward nose

Nose with noticeable stop

Very fine, satiny chocolate coat

Head slightly rounded at top and tapers to blunt wedge

Elegant, muscular body

Back level from shoulders to rump

Wide cheekbones

Strong jaw and chin

Lilac coat

Slender legs with small, oval paws

AMERICAN BURMESE

ALWAYS CRAVING COMPANY, THIS CAT IS FUN-SEEKING AND INTERESTED IN EVERYTHING

Place of origin Possibly Burma (Myanmar)

Date of origin 1930s

Breed registries CFA, TICA

Weight range 8-14lb (3.5-6.5kg)

Grooming

Colors and patterns
Brown (sable), chocolate (champagne), blue and lilac (platinum).

There are several conflicting accounts of how the Burmese cat came to the West. All that is known for certain is that a Southeast Asian cat of this type, belonging to a Dr. Thompson, appeared in the US in the 1930s and was used to found a new breed. The first recognized American Burmese cats were all a rich brown in color. Later, further colors were accepted, although not as many as in the European version of this breed, which also has a more Asian appearance. The Burmese is a lovely family pet that can never have enough company and attention.

Wide-set, round golden eyes

Visible break on nose

Ears with slightly rounded tips

Richly colored, close-lying lilac coat

Full, round face

Short, rounded muzzle

Underparts reveal lighter sepia patterning

Strong, compact body

Sturdy legs with round paws

MANDALAY

THIS GLOSSY-COATED BEAUTY WAS DEVELOPED FROM THE BURMESE CAT

Place of origin New Zealand
Date of origin 1980s
Breed registries FIFe
Weight range 8–14lb (3.5–6.5kg)
Grooming

Colors and patterns
Many solid colors and patterns, including tabby and tortoiseshell.

In the 1980s two breeders in New Zealand discovered independently that accidental matings between Burmese cats (p.39) and domestic cats produced promising kittens. From these litters, they both went on to develop what is now known as the Mandalay, which has the same breed standard as the Burmese but a greater variety of coat colors. Sleek, glossy, and golden eyed, this lovely cat is best known in its native country. The Mandalay is very alert and active, and its lithe frame is packed with muscle. It is warmly affectionate toward its own family but inclined to be cautious with strangers.

Large amber eyes slant toward nose

Tail tapers very slightly to rounded tip

Strong, round chest

Top of head is slightly rounded

Back level from shoulders to rump

Wide jaw and firm chin

Short, black, satiny coat

Neat, oval paws

TONKINESE

A CHIC AND SLEEK BUT STRONGLY MUSCLED CAT WITH PLENTY OF SUBSTANCE

Place of origin US

Date of origin 1950s

Breed registries CFA, GCCF, TICA

Weight range 6–12lb (2.5–5.5kg)

Grooming

Colors and patterns
All colors except cinnamon and fawn, in patterns including pointed, tabby, and tortoiseshell.

This breed was created by crossing Burmese with Siamese cats, which blends the coloring of both breeds but has a more compact body than many cats of Asian ancestry. It has achieved considerable popularity both in the US, where it was created, and in the UK. The Tonkinese has an independent spirit and would rule the household if it could, but it also has a loving nature and is gratifyingly eager to climb on laps. Playing games, socializing with other pets, and welcoming strangers to the home are all things that the Tonkinese is good at.

Slight snub to nose

Blunt muzzle

Brown shaded coat

High cheekbones

Darker brown legs, tail, and face

Round-tipped ears set to sides of head

Almond-shaped deep-colored eyes

Well-balanced body, neither long nor stocky

Sleek, close-lying chocolate tortoiseshell coat darkens with age

Patterning continues into belly

Slender legs with oval feet

ORIENTAL–WHITE

THIS DAINTY ARISTOCRATIC CAT HAS A SPARKLING WHITE COAT

Place of origin	UK
Date of origin	1950s
Breed registries	CFA, FIFe, GCCF, TICA
Weight range	9–14lb (4–6.5kg)

Grooming

Colors and patterns
White only.

Development of this breed began in the 1950s, with crosses between the Siamese and white shorthaired cats. In the UK the first of these hybrids had either orange or blue eyes, but selective breeding produced cats with blue eyes only, which were given the name of Foreign White. In the US, either green or blue eyes are permitted, and the cat is regarded as a solid-colored variant of the Oriental Shorthair, known as the Oriental White. This striking breed has the characteristic elongated lines and vibrant personality of the Siamese. Many blue-eyed white cats have a genetically linked tendency to deafness, but the Foreign White is free from this defect.

Almond-shaped blue eyes

Pink nose leather

Long, lithe body

Neat oval paws

Very large, pointed ears

Wedge-shaped, tapering head

Short, fine, close-lying white coat

Taut abdomen

Slender legs

ORIENTAL SOLID

THIS CAT WAS BRED TO COMBINE SIAMESE LINES WITH TRADITIONAL SOLID COLORS

Place of origin	UK
Date of origin	1950s
Breed registries	CFA, FIFe, GCCF, TICA
Weight range	9–14 lb (4–6.5 kg)

Grooming

Colors and patterns
Colors include brown (known as Havana), ebony, red, cream, lilac, and blue.

Solid-colored Oriental Shorthairs were developed in the 1950s, initially by crossing Siamese cats (pp.54–57) with other shorthaired cats to eliminate the typical Siamese colorpoint pattern. The first of the Oriental Shorthairs had coats in a rich dark shade of brown and were known as Havanas. In later years, these cats were used to develop a separate breed (p.52) in the US. Decades of further selective breeding introduced a wide range of other solid colors to the Oriental Shorthair, starting with a diluted version of the Havana referred to as lavender in the US and lilac in the UK.

Nose leather is pink

Lilac coat

Fine-boned but muscular body

Slightly slanting green eyes

Long, straight nose

Long, elegant neck

Color is uniform from root to tip of each hair

Hips should not be wider than shoulders

Red coat has satiny texture

Hindlegs longer than forelegs

ORIENTAL CINNAMON AND FAWN
THIS BEAUTIFUL CAT HAS TWO UNUSUAL COLOR VERSIONS

Place of origin	UK
Date of origin	1960s
Breed registries	CFA, FIFe, GCCF, TICA
Weight range	9–14 lb (4–6.5 kg)

Grooming

Colors and patterns
Cinnamon and fawn with no trace of white.

These variations of the Oriental Shorthair are rare because it has proved difficult for breeders to produce their subtle colors. The first Cinnamon was a kitten born in the 1960s to a male Abyssinian (p.83) and a female seal point Siamese (pp.54-55). The attractive and unusual shade of this kitten's coat—a lighter, reddish-tinged version of the rich brown Oriental solid-coloring known as Havana—inspired its breeder to develop a new line. Fawn Orientals, which were developed slightly later, are an even more diluted brown and their coats have a mushroom-pink or rosy tint, especially when seen in sunlight.

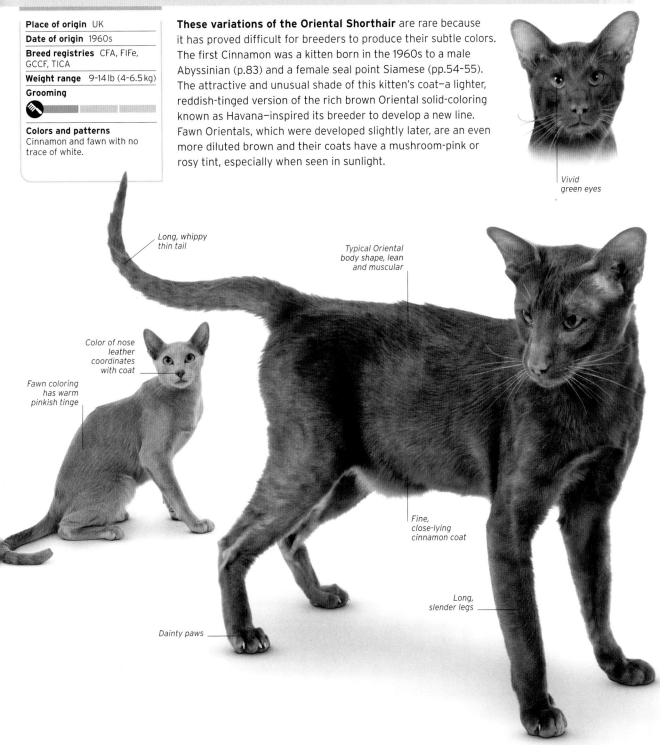

Vivid green eyes

Long, whippy thin tail

Typical Oriental body shape, lean and muscular

Color of nose leather coordinates with coat

Fawn coloring has warm pinkish tinge

Fine, close-lying cinnamon coat

Long, slender legs

Dainty paws

ORIENTAL–SMOKE

THIS STRIKING CAT IS NOT YET AS POPULAR AS OTHER ORIENTAL COLORS

Place of origin	UK
Date of origin	1970s
Breed registries	CFA, FIFe, GCCF, TICA
Weight range	9–14 lb (4–6.5 kg)

Grooming

Colors and patterns
Any Oriental solid colors in tortoiseshell and parti-color patterns.

In 1971, a cross between a shaded silver hybrid cat and a red-point Siamese produced a litter of kittens in mixed colors. One kitten, which had the coat pattern known as smoke, inspired breeders to create a new look of Oriental. Each hair of a Smoke's coat has two color bands. The top band may be either a solid color—including blue, black, red, and chocolate—or tortoiseshell; beneath this, the hair is very pale or white for at least one-third of its length. The pale hair shows through the darker color and is particularly noticeable when the cat moves.

Vivid green eyes slant down toward nose

Ghost tabby markings

Ears with rounded tips continue wedge-shaped line of head

Long, tapering tail

Black smoke coat is short, fine, and glossy

Slender, graceful neck

Hindlegs longer than forelegs

Taut belly

Legs with same color tone as face

ORIENTAL–SHADED

A DELICATELY PATTERNED CAT WITH AN UNUSUAL AND SUBTLE BEAUTY

Place of origin UK

Date of origin 1970s

Breed registries CFA, FIFe, GCCF, TICA

Weight range 9–14 lb (4–6.5 kg)

Grooming

Colors and patterns
All tabby patterns and colors, except white.

The chance mating between a chocolate-point Siamese (pp.54–55) and a Persian Chinchilla (p.140) produced a litter that included two kittens with shaded silver coats. This aroused breeders' interest, and so began the slow progress toward a new range of Oriental cats. In a shaded Oriental, the coat is essentially a modified tabby pattern, in which the darker markings occur only on the upper ends of the hairs. These markings—which can appear as ticked, spotted, mackerel, or classic tabby patterns—may be quite pronounced in kittens, but as the cat matures, the pattern becomes less distinct and in some cats is barely visible.

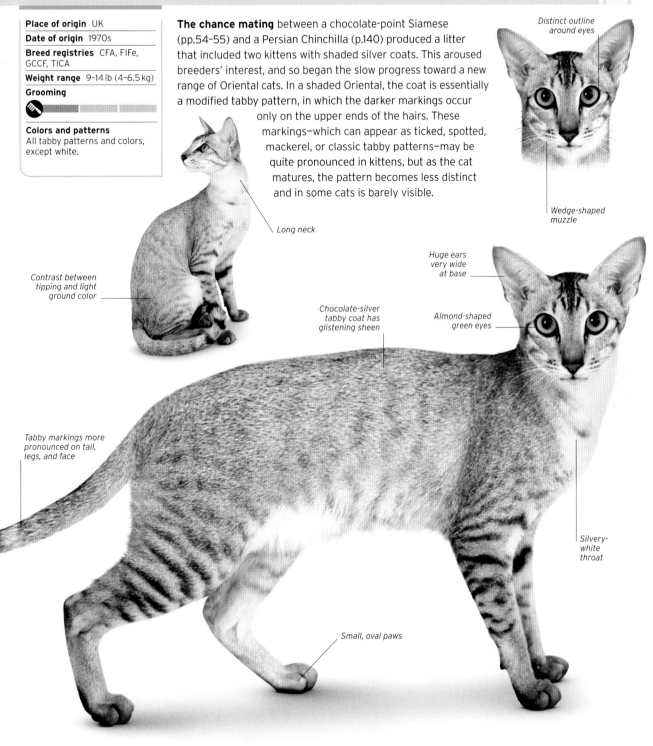

Distinct outline around eyes

Wedge-shaped muzzle

Long neck

Contrast between tipping and light ground color

Huge ears very wide at base

Almond-shaped green eyes

Chocolate-silver tabby coat has glistening sheen

Tabby markings more pronounced on tail, legs, and face

Silvery-white throat

Small, oval paws

ORIENTAL–TABBY

THIS LIVELY CAT COMBINES STREAMLINED LOOKS WITH A RANGE OF BEAUTIFUL TABBY PATTERNS

Place of origin UK

Date of origin 1970s

Breed registries CFA, FIFe, GCCF, TICA

Weight range 9–14 lb (4–6.5 kg)

Grooming

Colors and patterns
All colors and shades in tabby and patched-tabby patterns. Also with white.

Following the rising popularity of solid-colored Oriental Shorthairs, breeders turned their attention to producing a line of Oriental tabbies. Early attempts to introduce the tabby patterning to Orientals used crosses between nonpedigree tabbies and Siamese (pp.54–57). The first of these patterned Orientals, officially recognized in 1978, was a modern copy of the Siamese-type spotted tabbies believed to be the ancestors of today's domestic cats. By the 1980s, Orientals with ticked, mackerel, and classic tabby patterning in a wide variety of colors had also been developed. The patched-tabby Oriental, typically with patches of red or cream, was a further addition to the color palette.

Green eyes

Lines run from top of head to back of neck

Rich brown markings on pale bronze ground

Black tortoiseshell silver-spotted coat

Large, blotched markings on flanks

Chocolate classic tabby coat

Necklace markings

Dark rings on tail

Belly lighter in color

Barring on legs

ORIENTAL–TORTIE
THE PATTERNED COAT GIVES THIS CAT A PATCHWORK LOOK

Place of origin	UK
Date of origin	1960s
Breed registries	CFA, FIFe, GCCF, TICA
Weight range	9–14lb (4–6.5kg)

Grooming

Colors and patterns
Ground colors are black, blue, chocolate, lilac, fawn, cinnamon, and caramel; tortoiseshell pattern.

According to an illustrated manuscript, *The Cat Book Poems*, which may date back to the old kingdom of Siam (Thailand), tortie (tortoiseshell) patterned Oriental cats have a long history. Development of the modern Oriental Tortie began in the 1960s, with matings between solid-colored Orientals (p.44) and red, tortie, and cream-point Siamese (pp.54–55). The breed eventually gained official recognition in the 1980s. The Tortie coat comes in several ground colors mingled with contrasting patches of cream or red and cream, depending on the base color. Due to the distribution of tortoiseshell genes, torties are nearly always females; the rare males are usually sterile.

Head narrows to a fine muzzle

Random-patterned coat

Chocolate tortie coat is warm brown mixed with red shades

Green eyes

Thin, tapering tail

Firm, medium-sized body

Fine bone structure

Dainty, oval paws

ORIENTAL-BICOLOR

A LITHE AND SLENDER CAT WITH OFTEN DRAMATIC COLORING

Place of origin	US
Date of origin	1970s
Breed registries	FIFe, GCCF, TICA
Weight range	9-14 lb (4-6.5 kg)

Grooming

Colors and patterns
Various solid colors, shades, and patterns, including tabby, tortie, and some colorpoints, always with white areas.

Breeders in the US initially developed this exciting addition to the Oriental Shorthair group through crosses that included a Siamese (pp.54-57) and a bicolor American Shorthair (p.61). In Europe, further programs experimented with other crosses to achieve the right look. The first Oriental Bicolor in the UK arrived in 2004. This striking cat comes in a wonderful range of colors splashed over the coat in an endless variety of patterns; there is even a colorpointed, or Siamese, version. The breed standard requires the white patching to cover at least a third of the cat and to include the legs, underside, and muzzle.

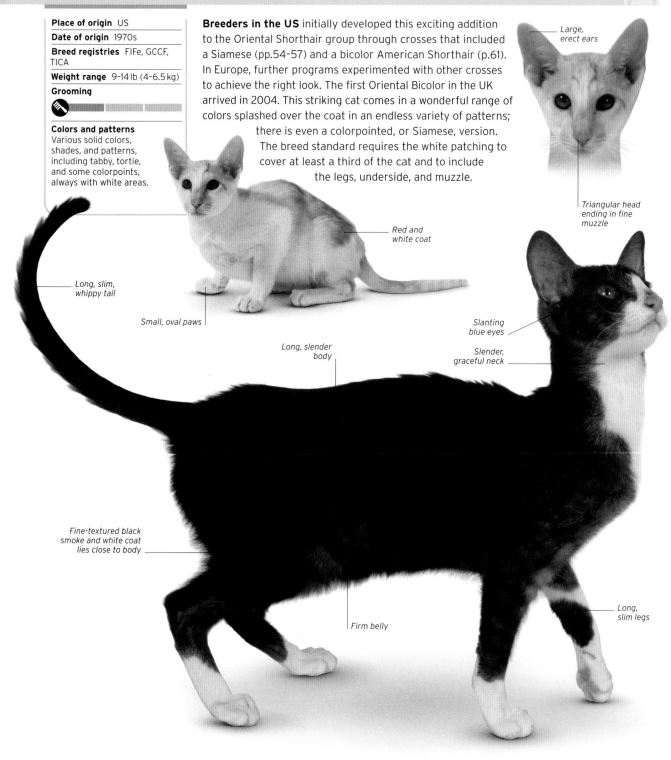

Large, erect ears

Triangular head ending in fine muzzle

Red and white coat

Long, slim, whippy tail

Small, oval paws

Long, slender body

Slanting blue eyes

Slender, graceful neck

Fine-textured black smoke and white coat lies close to body

Firm belly

Long, slim legs

HAVANA

A PLAYFUL, CHARMING, AND GENTLE CAT THAT ENJOYS AN INDOOR LIFE

Place of origin	US
Date of origin	1950s
Breed registries	CFA, TICA
Weight range	6-10 lb (2.5-4.5 kg)

Grooming

Colors and patterns
Rich brown and lilac.

A rare breed with a confusing background, the Havana (originally known as the Havana Brown) was developed originally to have two different looks, both with a rich brown coat. In the UK, the cat was produced through crosses with the Siamese (pp.54-57) and domestic shorthairs. This version, which had the long, lean Siamese conformation, was eventually classified as a solid-colored Oriental Shorthair (p.44). In the US, breeders did not use the Siamese, resulting in a cat with a rounder face and less elongated body (shown here). The stunning Havana is hard to ignore, but if it does not receive attention, it will certainly seek it. This affectionate cat likes to be close to people at all times.

Vivid green eyes

Muzzle narrows behind whiskers

Narrow head with rounded muzzle

Brown whiskers match coat color

Firm, well-muscled body

Large, round-tipped ears

Sleek, rich chestnut-brown coat with no other color markings

Brown nose leather has rosy tinge

Straight, slim legs with oval feet

SUFFOLK

AN INTELLIGENT, COMPANIONABLE BREED THAT MAKES AN EXCELLENT HOUSE CAT

Place of origin	UK
Date of origin	2014
Breed registries	GCCF
Weight range	6.5–11 lb (3–5 kg)

Grooming

Colors and patterns
Chocolate and lilac.

A relatively new breed, so called because the two original breeders live in the county of Suffolk, UK. In 2007, concerned by the changes that had occurred in modernizing the Havana (p.51) by outcrossing with Siamese cats (pp.54–57), they started to breed cats from carefully selected British bloodlines that exhibited the older, more traditional features of the Havana. Cats descended from these matings were later recognized as Suffolks in 2014 and have since received full championship status. Most Suffolk cats have sleek, shiny, chocolate brown fur, but very occasionally kittens with lilac fur are born due to the presence of two recessive alleles in the dilution gene (p.10).

Green eyes

Gently rounded snout

Ears with broad bases and rounded tips

Well-muscled body

Tail tapers slightly toward the tip

Long legs with oval-shaped paws

THAI

THIS VOCAL CAT LOVES PEOPLE AND EXPECTS LOTS OF ATTENTION

Place of origin Europe

Date of origin 1990s

Breed registries FIFe, GCCF, TICA

Weight range 6–12 lb (2.5–5.5 kg)

Grooming

Colors and patterns
Any point colors, including tabby and tortoiseshell, with pale ground color.

Lithe and elegant, with points that come in many colors, the Thai was bred to resemble the traditional Siamese cat of the 1950s, before it began to develop a more extreme, elongated appearance. The defining feature of the Thai is its head, which has a long, flat forehead; rounded cheeks; and a tapering, wedge-shaped muzzle. This cat is very active and intelligent, investigating everything and following its owner everywhere. It is good at communicating both vocally and in actions and will persist in getting a response. The breed is not suitable for a home where it will be left alone for long periods.

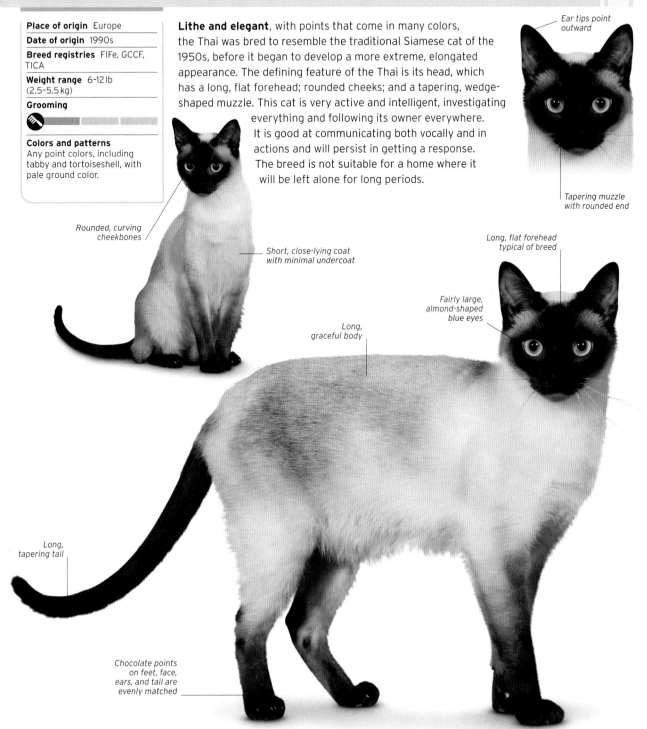

Ear tips point outward

Tapering muzzle with rounded end

Rounded, curving cheekbones

Short, close-lying coat with minimal undercoat

Long, flat forehead typical of breed

Fairly large, almond-shaped blue eyes

Long, graceful body

Long, tapering tail

Chocolate points on feet, face, ears, and tail are evenly matched

Very large, pointed ears continue line of head

Lean, elongated body

Almond-shaped blue eyes

Wedge-shaped head

Fine, short, close-lying ivory coat with cinnamon points

Straight nose

Neat, oval paws

Points on legs slightly lighter than on tail and head

Thin tail tapers to a point

Long, slender legs

SIAMESE–SELF-POINTED

THIS INSTANTLY RECOGNIZABLE BREED IS UNIQUE IN LOOKS AND PERSONALITY

Place of origin	Thailand (Siam)
Date of origin	14th century
Breed registries	CFA, FIFe, GCCF, TICA
Weight range	6–12 lb (2.5–5.5 kg)

Grooming

Colors and patterns
All solid colors in pointed patterns.

The history of the Siamese includes more myths and legends than hard facts, and the true tale of this Royal Cat of Siam is now lost in time. It is certainly thought to be a very old breed; a cat with dark points is pictured in *The Cat Book Poems*, a manuscript produced in Siam (now Thailand) that possibly dates back to the 14th century. The first Siamese cats definitely known in the West appeared at cat shows in London during the 1870s, and in that same decade, a cat was sent from Bangkok to the US as a gift for the First Lady.

In the breed's early years of development, on both sides of the Atlantic, all Siamese cats were seal points, and it was not until the 1930s that new colors—blue, chocolate, and lilac—were introduced, and later others were added. The appearance of the Siamese has also changed in other ways over the years. Traits such as crossed eyes and a kinked tail, which were once common in the Siamese, have been bred out and are now seen as

faults in terms of show standards. More controversially, modern breeding has taken the elongated body and narrow head of the Siamese to extremes, producing an ultra-lean and angular look. With a super-sized ego and a loud voice that it uses to demand attention, the Siamese is the most extroverted of all cats. This highly intelligent breed is full of fun and energy and makes a wonderful family pet, as ready to give affection as to receive it.

DEVELOPING COLORPOINTS

All Siamese kittens are born pure white. Their point colors emerge gradually and should be recognizable by around eight weeks. The color may take a year or more to develop its full depth.

SIAMESE–TABBY-POINTED

THIS FRIENDLY BREED IS A STUNNING VARIATION OF THE WORLD'S MOST FAMOUS CAT

Place of origin UK

Date of origin 1960s

Breed registries FIFe, GCCF, TICA

Weight range 6–12 lb (2.5–5.5 kg)

Grooming

Colors and patterns
Many tabby point colors, including seal, blue, chocolate, lilac, red, cream, cinnamon, caramel, fawn, and apricot; also various patched tabby point colors.

A few Siamese cats with tabby points are mentioned in early 20th-century records, but selective development of this new variation did not begin until the 1960s. The first tabby point Siamese to attract the attention of breeders is said to have been a kitten born to a solid-point female Siamese as a result of an unplanned mating. It was some years before the Siamese Tabby-Pointed was recognized and officially named as a breed in the UK; in the US, this cat is known as a Lynx Colorpoint. Originally, only seal tabbies appeared, but many other beautiful tabby colors have now been added to the breed standard.

Deep blue eyes

Nose leather pink with darker rim

Long, slender body

Dark-spotted whisker pads

Ears outlined in same color as mask

Well-defined tabby stripes on mask, including typical tabby "M" mark

Ivory-colored body with chocolate points

Tail has well-defined rings and solid-colored tip

Faint stripes on legs

SIAMESE–TORTIE-POINTED

MULTICOLORED POINTS ADD TO THE SPECIAL CHARM OF THIS SIAMESE

Place of origin UK
Date of origin 1960s
Breed registries GCCF, TICA
Weight range 6–12 lb
(2.5–5.5 kg)
Grooming

Colors and patterns
Various tortie point colors:
seal, blue, chocolate, lilac,
caramel, cinnamon, and fawn.

Producing tortie (tortoiseshell) colorpoints in the Siamese involves a complicated breeding process that introduces the gene for orange coloring. This gene causes random changes in solid colors such as seal, blue, or fawn, resulting in a mottled pattern in which shades of red, apricot, or cream are evident. In some variations, there may be striping as well. In kittens, the full mixture of colors emerges gradually and may take up to a year to develop fully. The Seal Tortie-Pointed was the first color to be granted official status as a Tortie Siamese in the UK in the late 1960s.

*Intensely
blue eyes*

*Delicate
muzzle*

*Long,
whippy tail*

*Large, pricked
ears follow
contours of head*

*Slender,
graceful body*

*Color of nose leather
coordinates with points*

*Colorpoints
contrast with
ivory-colored body*

*Pale coat with
seal tortie points*

*Each tortie
point is broken
up with cream*

COLORPOINT SHORTHAIR

A LOVING, PLAYFUL CAT WITH A LOOK-AT-ME ATTITUDE

Place of origin US
Date of origin 1940s/1950s
Breed registries CFA
Weight range 6–12 lb (2.5–5.5 kg)
Grooming

Colors and patterns
Various solid,
tabby, and lynx
point colors.

Developed specifically for its beautiful color combinations, this breed was created during the 1940s and '50s, initially by crossing a Siamese with a red tabby American Shorthair (p.61). If not for its different range of colors, the Colorpoint Shorthair would be impossible to distinguish from the Siamese, because it possesses the same elongated body, slender head, oversized ears, and brilliant blue eyes as its relative. Intelligent, sociable, and highly vocal, this cat likes to be the center of attention. A Colorpoint Shorthair needs family life—the more fun going on, the better—and is not suitable for owners who are out of the home for long periods.

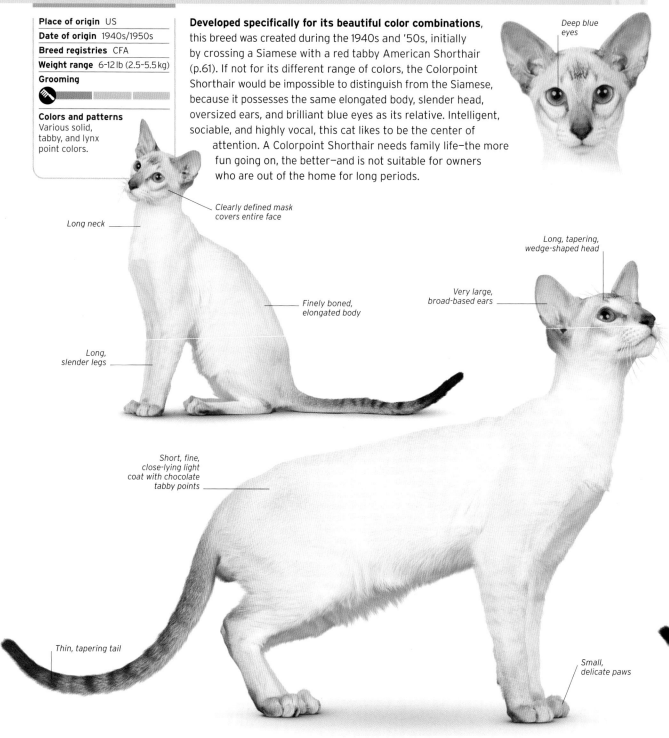

Deep blue eyes

Clearly defined mask covers entire face

Long neck

Finely boned, elongated body

Long, slender legs

Long, tapering, wedge-shaped head

Very large, broad-based ears

Short, fine, close-lying light coat with chocolate tabby points

Thin, tapering tail

Small, delicate paws

SEYCHELLOIS

THIS CAT IS NOT FOR OWNERS WHO LIKE A QUIET LIFE

Place of origin UK

Date of origin 1980s

Breed registries FIFe

Weight range 9–14 lb (4–6.5 kg)

Grooming

Colors and patterns
White ground color with solid, tortie, and lynx contrast markings. Always in bicolor and pointed pattern.

This comparatively new breed was specially created in the UK to resemble the distinctively patterned cats found in the Seychelles, although it is not seen these days. The first crosses were between a Siamese (pp.54–57) and a calico Persian (p.152); later, Oriental cats were added to the breeding program, and the mix produced a graceful, long-headed, big-eared cat in both shorthaired and longhaired versions. According to the extent of its dramatic color markings, the Seychellois is classified into three types, known as neuviéme (with the least color), septiéme, and huitiéme (with the largest color patches). With a reputation for flightiness, the Seychellois is said to be a demanding, although highly affectionate, companion.

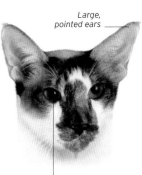

Large, pointed ears

Deep blue, almond-shaped eyes

Wedge-shaped head with long, straight nose

Short, shiny coat with minimal undercoat

Strongly contrasting seal huitiéme markings

Long neck

Slim, elongated body with chocolate septiéme markings on coat

Long, thin, darker-colored tail

Long, slender, strongly muscled legs

Small, white, oval paws

SNOWSHOE

THIS WELL-NAMED COLORPOINTED CAT HAS DISTINCTIVE SPARKLING WHITE FEET

Place of origin	US
Date of origin	1960s
Breed registries	FIFe, GCCF, TICA
Weight range	6–12 lb (2.5–5.5 kg)

Grooming

Colors and patterns
Typical Siamese colors in pointed pattern, with white feet. Blue or seal most common.

The white feet that define the Snowshoe were originally a "mistake," first seen in a litter of kittens born to a normal colorpoint Siamese. Their breeder, Dorothy Hinds-Daugherty of Philadelphia, liked them enough to develop the striking new look, using crosses between Siamese (pp.54–57) and the American Shorthair (p.61) to produce the Snowshoe. Intelligent, responsive, and full of character, these cats love a home atmosphere and usually prefer to keep their family in sight. Most Snowshoes get along very well with other cats. Their steady temperament makes them a good choice for first-time cat owners.

Straight nose

High, rounded cheekbones

Light-colored coat with seal colorpoints

Slightly rounded, wedge-shaped head

Large, broad-based ears have rounded tips

Walnut-shaped blue eyes

Close-lying, blue point coat with no undercoat

Long, athletic body

Long, white mittens on hind paws should be evenly matched

Oval paws

AMERICAN SHORTHAIR

A ROBUST, EASY-CARE CAT THAT IS RECOGNIZED IN A HUGE RANGE OF COLORS

Place of origin US

Date of origin 1890s

Breed registries CFA, TICA

Weight range 8–15 lb (3.5–7 kg)

Grooming

Colors and patterns
Most solid colors and shades; patterns include bicolor, tabby, and tortoiseshell.

The first domestic cats in the US are said to have arrived with the early pilgrims in the 1600s. Over the following centuries, sturdy, workmanlike cats spread all over America, most of them kept as efficient mousers rather than as house pets. But by the beginning of the 20th century, a more refined form of the barnyard hunter, known as the Domestic Shorthair, began to emerge. Careful breeding further improved the Domestic, and by the 1960s—now renamed the American Shorthair—it was attracting attention at pedigree cat shows. Healthy and hardy, American Shorthairs are perfect family cats that fit in with almost any type of household.

Broad, rounded head

Square muzzle and strong jaws

Large head with full face

Ears slightly rounded at tips

Short, thick, resilient coat

Round paws with heavy pads

Classic silver tabby coat

Well-developed, powerful body

Tail tapers to blunt end

Straight, muscular legs

EUROPEAN SHORTHAIR

A FINE DOMESTIC CAT WITH AN AIR OF QUALITY

Place of origin	Sweden
Date of origin	1980s
Breed registries	FIFe
Weight range	8–15 lb (3.5–7 kg)
Grooming	

Colors and patterns
Various colors and bicolors in solid and smoke. Patterns include colorpoint, tabby, and tortoiseshell.

At first glance, the European Shorthair looks very much like a typical house cat. Largely popular in Scandinavia, it was developed in Sweden from ordinary domestic cats, but careful breeding programs ensured that only the best foundation stock, selected for quality of color and conformation, were used. Unlike most cats of similar type, including the British Shorthair, this breed has not been outcrossed to other lines. Robust and sturdily built, the European Shorthair is a dependable pet that thrives both indoors and out. It is sociable but retains an air of independence and can be a little aloof with strangers.

Blue eyes

Large, round face with well-developed cheeks

Nose straight and fairly broad

Thick, springy, cream-colored coat

Firm, rounded paws

Ears may be tufted

Muscular neck

Medium-length, well-muscled, and sturdy body

Very dense coat with blue shading

Rounded chest

Tail thick at base

Darkest blue pointing on tail

Strong legs with even blue coloring extending to paws

CHARTREUX

A CHUNKY BUT AGILE BREED WITH A "SMILEY" EXPRESSION

Place of origin	France
Date of origin	Pre-18th century
Breed registries	CFA, FIFe, TICA
Weight range	7–17 lb (3–7.5 kg)

Grooming

Colors and patterns
Blue-gray only.

Just how far back the history of this very old French breed goes is open to debate. The Chartreux was first named in the mid-18th century, and some legends link it to the Carthusian monks, makers of the renowned Chartreuse liqueur, though there is no proof that they ever kept woolly coated blue cats like this one. With its calm, undemanding personality and soft voice, this breed is an unobtrusive yet affectionate house cat. It enjoys quiet play and occasionally explodes in a burst of extra energy when in a hunting mode.

Round head with full cheeks

Narrow, tapering muzzle with "smiling" expression

Blue-gray nose straight with slight stop

Short, dense blue-gray coat

Round golden eyes

Short neck

Weather-resistant coat is slightly woolly in texture

Blue lips

Body solid and muscular but not stocky

Sturdy, fine-boned legs

RUSSIAN BLUE

FRIENDLY BUT SELF-SUFFICIENT, THIS GRACEFUL CAT DOES NOT DEMAND MUCH ATTENTION

Place of origin Russia

Date of origin Pre-19th century

Breed registries CFA, FIFe, GCCF, TICA

Weight range 7–12lb (3–5.5kg)

Grooming

Colors and patterns
Blue of various shades.

The most widely accepted version of this breed's ancestry suggests that it originated around the Russian port of Archangel, just below the Arctic Circle. Supposedly brought to Europe by sailors, the Russian Blue was attracting interest in the UK well before the end of the 19th century, and had also appeared in North America by the early 20th century. With its gracious air and beautiful plush blue coat, it is not surprising that the Russian Blue is now highly popular. Reserved with strangers, this cat has an abundance of quiet affection to give its owners. Differently colored types of the breed have been developed under the name Russian Shorthair.

Dense fur gives a broad-faced appearance

Straight nose

Thick, plush blue coat

Long, tapering tail

Long, finely boned legs

Long, lithe body

Relatively large, wide-set ears, very thin at tips

Bright green eyes

Silver-tipped guard hairs

Small, rounded paws

PLUSH FUR
The Russian Blue's coat, with its rich pile and silvery sheen, is a distinguishing feature of the breed. This kitten is still at the cute stage, but as an adult he will combine grace with dignity.

Large, powerful body

Short, dense black coat with no white markings

Small ears set wide apart

Large, round golden eyes

Short, strong neck

Massive head with full cheeks

Firm, round paws

Medium-short, strongly boned legs

Tail tapers slightly

BRITISH SHORTHAIR–SOLID

A CAT THAT COMBINES GOOD LOOKS WITH AN EASYGOING TEMPERAMENT

Place of origin	UK
Date of origin	1800s
Breed registries	CFA, FIFe, GCCF, TICA
Weight range	9–18 lb (4–8 kg)

Grooming

Colors and patterns
All solid colors.

Originally developed from the best examples of ordinary British domestic cats, the British Shorthair was one of the first pedigree cats to appear in shows during the late 19th century. In the following decades, the Shorthair was all but eclipsed by longhaired cats, particularly the Persian, but survived by a narrow margin to enjoy a revival from the mid-20th century onward.

A descendant of cats that worked for their living, keeping down vermin on farms and homesteads, the British Shorthair is now something of a blueprint for the perfect fireside cat. The breed is highly popular in Europe and is steadily gaining a following in the US, where it is less well-known.

Many decades of careful selection have produced a well-proportioned cat of superb quality. Powerfully built, the British Shorthair has a medium to large, tightly knit body carried on sturdy legs. The massive, round head; broad cheeks; and large, open eyes are characteristic features

of the breed. The British Shorthair has a short, dense coat that comes in a variety of colors and has a deep pile and firm texture.

In temperament, this cat is as calm and friendly as its chubby-cheeked, placid expression appears to suggest. It can be kept equally well as a town or country cat. Strong, but not athletic or hyperactive, a British Shorthair prefers to keep its paws on the ground and is perfectly happy to stay indoors and commandeer the sofa. However, it also enjoys time outside and readily uses the hunting skills that made its ancestors such an asset in the past.

Quietly affectionate, the Shorthair likes to stay near its owner. Although alert to what is going on in the household, this cat it is not overdemanding of attention.

British Shorthairs generally have robust health and can be long-lived. They are easy to care for, because the thick coat does not mat or tangle and regular combing is all that is required to keep it in good condition.

BRITISH SHORTHAIR–COLORPOINTED

SIAMESE-TYPE COLORS ADD A NEW LOOK TO THIS TRADITIONAL BREED

Place of origin UK

Date of origin 1800s

Breed registries FIFe, GCCF, TICA

Weight range 9–18 lb (4–8 kg)

Grooming

Colors and patterns
Various point colors, including blue-cream, seal, red, chocolate, and lilac; also with lynx and tortie patterns.

The most recent of the British Shorthair variations, the Colorpoint was recognized only in 1991. This unusual cat is the result of experimental crossbreeding to produce a British Shorthair with the pointed coat pattern of the Siamese. Various attractive colors have been developed and, like the Siamese, all types have blue eyes, although the stocky build and round head typical of the Shorthair remain unchanged. Because of the similarities in name, the British Shorthair Colorpoint is sometimes confused with an Oriental-type American breed called the Colorpoint Shorthair (p.58).

Blue-cream
tortie mask

Pale
ground
color with
blue-cream
highlights

Chunky body

Round
blue eyes

Typically full,
rounded face

Powerful
shoulders

Short neck

Tortie pattern
more evident
on tail

Blue points
broken with
cream markings

BRITISH SHORTHAIR–BICOLOR

THIS HANDSOME CAT IS BOLDLY MARKED WITH COLOR PATCHES

Place of origin	UK
Date of origin	1800s
Breed registries	CFA, FIFe, GCCF, TICA
Weight range	9–18 lb (4–8 kg)

Grooming

Colors and patterns
Black and white, blue and white, red and white, and cream and white.

Black and white British Shorthairs were much valued in the 19th century, when this breed had its beginnings, but they were never common. The Bicolor as it is today, which comes in several combinations of white and another color, was not fully developed until the 1960s. At that time, almost impossibly high breeding standards required the color patches to be distributed over head and body with complete symmetry. The rules have since been relaxed, but the best Bicolors still have strikingly even markings.

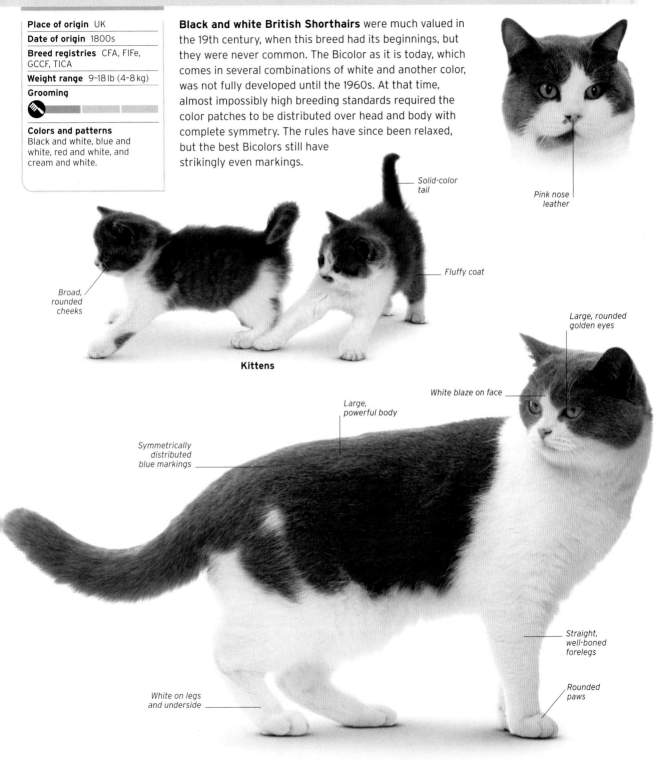

Pink nose leather

Solid-color tail

Fluffy coat

Broad, rounded cheeks

Kittens

Large, rounded golden eyes

White blaze on face

Large, powerful body

Symmetrically distributed blue markings

Straight, well-boned forelegs

Rounded paws

White on legs and underside

CALM CHARACTER
This British Shorthair kitten, dozing off mid-game, already shows the rounded cheeks that are one of the breed's characteristics. Although amiable, the Shorthair enjoys its own company.

BRITISH SHORTHAIR–SMOKE

THIS BREED'S HIDDEN SILVER UNDERCOAT CREATES A DISTINCTIVE EFFECT

Place of origin	UK
Date of origin	1800s
Breed registries	CFA, FIFe, GCCF, TICA
Weight range	9–18 lb (4–8 kg)

Grooming

Colors and patterns
Smoke pattern in all solid colors and in tortoiseshell and pointed patterns.

A Smoke cat can look as though it is just one color until it moves or its fur is parted to reveal a narrow silver band at the base of the hairs. This is the effect of the silver gene, which inhibits the development of color in the coat, and which British Shorthair Smokes inherited from the silver tabbies in their ancestry. Smoke coloration is even more subtly attractive in the tortoiseshell version, which has two colors in the topcoat.

Round orange eyes

Black nose leather

Ears rounded at tips

Rounded forehead

Prominent whisker pads

Tail tapers to rounded tip

Large, firm, rounded paws

Deep chest

Black smoke topcoat conceals silver undercoat

Strong, medium to short legs

BRITISH SHORTHAIR–TABBY

AN OLD FAVORITE THAT HAS BEEN DEVELOPED IN A VARIETY OF ATTRACTIVE COLORS

Place of origin UK

Date of origin 1800s

Breed registries CFA, FIFe, GCCF, TICA

Weight range 9–18 lb (4–8 kg)

Grooming

Colors and patterns
All traditional tabby patterns with many colors, including silver variations; patched tabby in various colors, including silver variations.

Although the British Shorthair is the most even-tempered of cats, this variation is a reminder of its wild tabby-patterned ancestors. Brown tabbies were among the first British Shorthairs to appear in cat shows in the 1870s, and red and silver versions became popular early on in the breed's history. This cat now comes in a wide range of additional colors, with three traditional tabby patterns: classic (or blotched) tabby, with markings arranged in broad whorls; mackerel, with narrower markings; and spotted. In the patched tabby, the coat has a second ground color.

Typical tabby "M" mark on forehead

Brick-red nose leather

Black silver tabby coat

Narrow markings on cheeks

Large, round golden eyes

Red classic tabby coat

Even, unbroken rings on tail

Ground color even over whole body

Legs barred with darker bracelets

Necklace of stripes around neck

BRITISH SHORTHAIR—TIPPED

A DELICATELY COLORED CAT WITH A SPARKLE TO ITS COAT

Place of origin	UK
Date of origin	1800s
Breed registries	CFA, FIFe, GCCF, TICA
Weight range	9–18 lb (4–8 kg)

Grooming

Colors and patterns
Various, including black-tipped on white or golden undercoat; red-tipped on white undercoat.

In a tipped cat, a pale undercoat is overlaid with what appears to be a light dusting of color. This effect is produced by the ends of the top hairs being colored to about one-eighth of their length. The Tipped British Shorthair—originally called the Chinchilla Shorthair—comes in various color forms. These include silver (white undercoat with black tipping), golden (warm golden or apricot undercoat with black tipping), and the rare Shell Cameo (white undercoat with red tipping), which is known as red in the UK.

Rounded muzzle

Red skin encircles copper-colored eyes

Black tipping distributed over back, flanks, and head

Red nose leather outlined with black

White underparts contrast with red-tipped coat

Small to medium-sized ears

Legs lightly tipped

Black-tipped coat

Short, thick neck

Black-tipped tail with white underside

Body deep in flanks

BRITISH SHORTHAIR–TORTIE

MINGLED COLORS GIVE THIS CAT'S COAT AN UNUSUAL MARBLED APPEARANCE

Place of origin	UK
Date of origin	1800s
Breed registries	CFA, FIFe, GCCF, TICA
Weight range	9–18 lb (4–8 kg)

Grooming

Colors and patterns
Blue-cream, chocolate, lilac, or black tortoiseshell (with white patches in the calico).

In a tortoiseshell (tortie), two coat colors are softly blended. There are many variations, but the most common is black mixed with red—the first tortie color to be developed in British Shorthairs. Blue-cream tortoiseshell, in which black is replaced by blue and red by cream, is another of the older colors, recognized since the 1950s. In the Calico (known as Tortie and White in the UK), the colors are more clearly defined as patches. For genetic reasons, torties are nearly always female and the few males are sterile.

Deep orange eyes

White markings cover a third of the body

White paws

Areas of tortie patterning clearly defined

Red and black color areas intermingle evenly

Dense tortie coat

Short, level back

Ears broad at base

Slight dip in nose

Broad chest

Rounded paws

TURKISH SHORTHAIR

A LITTLE-KNOWN BREED THAT IS AFFECTIONATE AND EASYGOING WITH PEOPLE

Place of origin	Turkey
Date of origin	pre-1700s
Breed registries	Other
Weight range	7–19lb (3–8.5kg)

Grooming

Colors and patterns
All colors except chocolate, cinnamon, lilac, and fawn, and all patterns except pointed.

The history of the Turkish Shorthair is uncertain, but this cat occurs naturally in various regions of Turkey and has probably existed there for a considerable time. Also known as the Anatolian or Anatoli, and the Anadolu Kedisi in Turkey, the breed is similar to the longer-haired Turkish Van cat (p.176). The Turkish Shorthair is rare even in its native country, but breeders, particularly in Germany and the Netherlands, are working to increase its numbers. This strong, agile cat has a great liking for playing in or with water and is known to enjoy a bath.

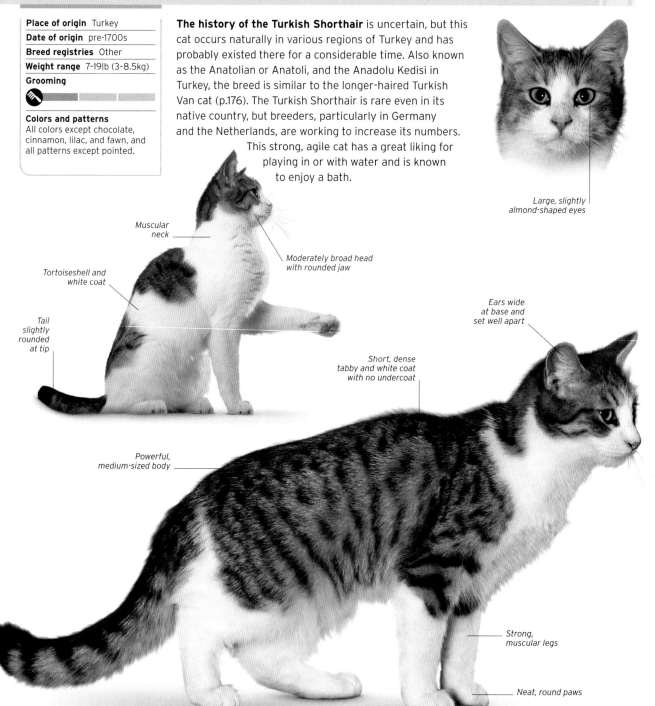

Large, slightly almond-shaped eyes

Muscular neck

Moderately broad head with rounded jaw

Tortoiseshell and white coat

Tail slightly rounded at tip

Ears wide at base and set well apart

Short, dense tabby and white coat with no undercoat

Powerful, medium-sized body

Strong, muscular legs

Neat, round paws

OJOS AZULES

THIS RARE AND ENIGMATIC BREED IS A NEWCOMER ON THE PEDIGREE CAT SCENE

Place of origin	US
Date of origin	1980s
Breed registries	TICA
Weight range	9–12lb (4–5.5kg)

Grooming

Colors and patterns
All colors and patterns.

First discovered in New Mexico in 1984, the Ojos Azules (the name means blue eyes in Spanish) is one of the rarest cats in the world. The stunning eye color is particularly unusual in that it appears with any coat color or pattern, in one or both eyes, including in the longhaired version. Development of the breed has been slow due to health problems that seem to occur when the gene for blue eyes is inherited from both parents. Hence the outcross to other non blue-eyed cats. A pretty and graceful cat, the Ojos Azules is said to be affectionate and friendly.

Nose has slight stop

Triangular head with prominent cheekbones

Sweet expression

Fine, silky white coat with black and red tortie markings

Different colored eyes

Ears set relatively high on head

Square muzzle

Tapering tail with extensive tortie markings

Hindlegs slightly longer than forelegs

EGYPTIAN MAU

STRIKINGLY PATTERNED, THIS IS THE ONLY NATURALLY SPOTTED DOMESTIC BREED

Place of origin Egypt

Date of origin 1950s

Breed registries CFA, FIFe, GCCF, TICA

Weight range 6–11 lb (2.5–5 kg)

Grooming

Colors and patterns
Bronze and silver in spotted tabby pattern. Black smoke has ghost tabby markings.

This cat bears a certain resemblance to the long-bodied, spotted cats seen in the tomb paintings of Ancient Egyptian pharaohs, but it cannot claim direct descent. The modern Egyptian Mau was developed by Natalie Troubetzkoy, a Russian princess in exile, who in 1956 imported several spotted Egyptian cats to the US from Italy. Here, the number of breeding cats remained small for many years until new imports late in the 20th century reinvigorated the gene pool. Maus are affectionate cats but are also inclined to be sensitive and shy. They need thoughtful socializing at an early age and are probably best suited to an experienced cat owner. However, once a Mau bonds with its family, it stays devoted for life.

Medium-long, wedge-shaped head

Large, almond-shaped green eyes

Broad-based, fairly large ears

Bronze spotted tabby coat

Forehead has typical tabby "M" marking

Spots on coat are random

Hindlegs longer than forelegs

Loose flap of skin between flank and hindleg

Broken necklace patterns on upper chest and neck

Small, slightly oval feet

RARE BEAUTY
A silver Egyptian Mau stalks through long grass, huge green eyes fixed on a possible target. This stunning spotted cat, which comes in three recognized colors, is extremely rare.

ARABIAN MAU

A DESERT CAT THAT IS WELL ADAPTED TO HOME LIFE

Place of origin United Arab Emirates

Date of origin 2000s (modern breed)

Breed registries Other

Weight range 7–15lb (3–7kg)

Grooming

Colors and patterns
Various solid colors and patterns, including tabby and bicolor.

A breed native to the Arabian Peninsula, this cat was a desert dweller that migrated to city streets when human populations encroached on its habitat. In 2004 breeding programs to develop the Arabian Mau were started, with the aim of preserving the cat's original traits and natural hardiness. With its high energy levels and need for mental stimulation, this breed can be a handful and will not be content to spend much time lazing around. However, the Arabian Mau is both loyal and affectionate, and sympathetic owners usually find it a highly rewarding pet.

Prominent whisker pads

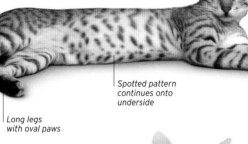

Slightly slanted, oval eyes

Spotted pattern continues onto underside

Long legs with oval paws

Large, pointed ears

Nose slightly concave

Necklace markings

White solid coat

Medium to large, muscular body

Banding on legs

Single mackerel tabby coat has firm texture

ABYSSINIAN

THIS SLINKY, GRACEFUL CAT IS FULL OF ENERGY AND NEEDS SPACE TO PLAY AND EXPLORE

Place of origin Ethiopia

Date of origin 19th century

Breed registries CFA, FIFe, GCCF, TICA

Weight range 9–17lb (4–7.5kg)

Grooming

Colors and patterns
Several color forms, all with distinct ticking and facial markings.

There are various accounts of the Abyssinian's history, including the attractive but highly improbable story that it descends from the sacred cats of Ancient Egypt. A more plausible version suggests that its forerunners might have been brought back from Abyssinia (now Ethiopia) by British soldiers when the Abyssinian War ended in the late 1860s. What is certain is that the modern breed was developed in the UK, most likely by crossing the British Shorthair (pp.68–77) with a more unusual, and possibly imported, breed. With its athletic build, aristocratic bearing, and beautiful ticked coat, the Abyssinian is a striking cat with a hint of wild about it. Intelligent and affectionate, Abyssinians make wonderful companions but they like an all-action life.

Rounded muzzle with prominent whisker pads

Distinctive dark facial markings around eyes

Silky, lustrous, usual coat

Eyes outlined in black

Large, alert ears set wide apart

Well-balanced, graceful body

Fine-textured blue coat

All hairs on coat are ticked with contrasting color bands

Lighter underparts

Long, tapering tail

Slender legs

Relatively small paws

AUSTRALIAN MIST

THIS AFFECTIONATE CAT HAS A STEADY TEMPERAMENT AND A DELICATELY BEAUTIFUL COAT

Place of origin Australia
Date of origin 1970s
Breed registries GCCF, TICA
Weight range 8–13lb (3.5–6kg)
Grooming

Colors and patterns
Spotted or marbled tabby, misted by ticking; colors include brown, blue, peach, chocolate, lilac, and gold.

The first pedigree cat to be developed in Australia, this breed was created from crosses between Burmese (pp.39–40), Abyssinian (p.83), and Australian domestic shorthair cats. Formerly known as the Spotted Mist, it comes in a range of attractive spotted and marbled patterns and colors, all enhanced by ticking that produces a delicate misted effect. The Australian Mist is extremely popular in its native country and has earned a reputation as a particularly easy pet to keep. It has a loving nature, lives happily indoors, and is equally suitable as a playmate for children or a faithful companion for the less active owner.

Prominent whisker pads

Short, sleek coat

Broad, rounded chest

Medium-large, firm body

Broad, slightly rounded head

Ears wide at base and tilt slightly forward

Green eyes with straight upper lids

Nose broad with slight dip

Blue marble tabby coat

Long tail thick in proportion to body

Paler underparts

Broken necklace markings

Neat oval paws

CEYLON

A FINE-BONED AND ELEGANT CAT WITH AN ATTRACTIVELY MARKED COAT

Place of origin	Sri Lanka
Date of origin	1980s
Breed registries	Other
Weight range	9–17lb (4–7.5kg)
Grooming	

Colors and patterns
Manila (black-ticked on sandy-gold ground color); various other markings and tickings, including blue, red, cream, and tortoiseshell.

Named after its native home (now Sri Lanka), the Ceylon was imported to Italy in the early 1980s, where the breed was developed. It is now found worldwide and, if not as widely known as other breeds, has achieved some popularity in Italy. With its beautiful ticked coat and sandy coloring, this cat is similar in appearance to the Abyssinian (p.83), though the two are not related. The Ceylon has a distinctive pattern on its forehead called the cobra mark, which is much valued. Breeders praise the cat's friendly nature and its responsiveness to attention.

Distinctive cobra mark on forehead

Darker lines on cheeks and forehead

Yellowish green eyes with dark rims

Large ears set high on head

Well-defined stripes on legs

Necklace markings around throat

Kitten

Sandy-colored, black-ticked coat

Clearly defined ticking on body

Broad chest

Short, fine-haired coat with minimal undercoat

Fine-boned but muscular legs

STRENGTH AND ELEGANCE
An Ocicat is a natural athlete, and the power in its graceful frame becomes evident when the cat is in motion. The sleek, spotted coat fits closely over smoothly gliding muscles.

OCICAT

AN ADAPTABLE AND CONFIDENT CAT THAT OFTEN RESPONDS WELL TO TRAINING

Place of origin US

Date of origin 1960s

Breed registries CFA, FIFe, GCCF, TICA

Weight range 6–14 lb (2.5–6.5 kg)

Grooming

Colors and patterns
Black, brown, blue, lilac, and fawn in spotted tabby pattern.

Despite its name, this spotted beauty is not a cross between the domestic cat and the ocelot—the native jungle cat of South and Central America—but it looks as though it ought to be. The Ocicat was actually the surprise product of an attempt in 1964 to breed a Siamese (pp.54–57) with colorpoints that matched the ticked coat of the Abyssinian (p.83). The first spotted kitten that appeared was kept solely as a pet, but others produced later were used to create the new breed. The inclusion of American Shorthairs (p.61) in the Ocicat's development program introduced greater size and substance. Ocicats have a delightful temperament, love company, and are easy to manage.

Broad, slightly square muzzle

Silver-spotted tabby coat

Characteristic tabby "M" mark on forehead

Large, almond-shaped eyes with dark rims

Lighter markings around eyes and on chin

Dark lines on cheeks

Powerful, athletic body

Darkest coloration appears on tip of tail

Short, shiny chocolate tabby coat marked with "thumbprint" spots

Necklace pattern around neck

Long, slightly tapering tail

Oval paws

AZTEC

A LARGE, BEAUTIFULLY MARKED TABBY WITH AN EXOTIC DIFFERENCE

Place of origin US

Date of origin 1960s

Breed registries GCCF

Weight range 6–14lb (2.5–6.5kg)

Grooming

Colors and patterns
Classic tabby pattern in various colors, including silver.

Previously known as the Ocicat Classic, this is a version of the Ocicat with markings in the classic tabby pattern rather than spots, this cat was recognized as a separate breed only comparatively recently, and is still not yet accepted as such by all breed authorities. The Aztec has the same history as its spotted cousin (pp.88–89), being a mixture of Siamese (pp.54–57), Abyssinian (pp.83–85), and American Shorthair (p.61). It is an energetic cat, with an enthusiasm for games and getting up onto high places. The breed has an excellent temperament and is highly sociable. An Aztec will not stay happy for long on its own, and is best-suited to a house full of people and action.

Large, broad-based ears

Long, broad muzzle

Large, almond-shaped eyes are angled slightly toward base of ears

Dark tabby markings on ticked brown fur

Tail has dark rings along its length

Traditional tabby "M" marking on forehead

Unbroken line of dark color runs from shoulders along spine

Large, lithe, well-muscled body

Evenly spaced bracelet markings on legs

SOKOKE

THIS CAT HAS A PEACEFUL NATURE BUT IS POSSESSIVE OF HOME AND FAMILY

Place of origin Kenya

Date of origin 1970s (modern breed)

Breed registries FIFe, GCCE, TICA

Weight range 8–14lb (3.5–6.5kg)

Grooming

Colors and patterns Ticked brown tabby only.

A native of the coastal Arabuko Sokoke Forest in Kenya, this spectacular tabby was discovered in the late 1970s, when a British Kenyan resident adopted two feral kittens with distinctive markings and used them for breeding. Sokokes were later imported to Europe and the US, and new bloodlines were introduced in the 21st century. The modern Sokoke combines the traits of what are known as the Old and New Lines. These cats develop close family bonds, and some have a natural talent for communicating vocally with their owners. They remain fairly active beyond kittenhood and enjoy playing games.

Eyes outlined with black

Prominent whisker pads

Long, slender, fine-boned legs

Classic tabby pattern on coat is blurred by ticking

Large, broad-based, upright ears

Black tip to tail

Skull almost flat at top

Long, whippy tail has firm feel

Chinstrap marking on throat

Long hindlegs give a tiptoe gait

CALIFORNIA SPANGLED

THIS CAT WITH EXOTIC JUNGLE LOOKS HAS A FAR FROM FIERCE PERSONALITY

Place of origin	US
Date of origin	1970s
Breed registries	None
Weight range	9–15lb (4–7kg)
Grooming	

Colors and patterns
Spotted tabby; ground colors include silver, bronze, gold, red, blue, black, brown, charcoal, and white.

This designer cat is a miniature reproduction of wild cats such as the leopard and ocelot. It was created by a conservation enthusiast, Paul Casey, to discourage the killing of wild animals for their fur. Casey reasoned that if people related spotted fur to their own pet cats, they would be against the destruction of wildlife in the name of fashion. The California Spangled was bred by using a variety of domestic cats, and has no wild cat species in its makeup. Hunting and playing are what this active cat enjoys most, but it is also sociable, affectionate, and easy to handle. It is not currently being bred.

Slightly rounded forehead

Wide cheekbones

Prominent whisker pads

Well-defined spots of various shapes, including round, blocked, and oval

Eyes slightly angled toward outer edge of ear

Gold spotted tabby coat has soft, velvety texture

Ears set high on head

Tail has dark rings and dark tip

Dark bars on legs

Long, lean, muscular body

TOYGER

THIS COMPANIONABLE AND INTELLIGENT BREED IS A STUNNINGLY BEAUTIFUL DESIGNER CAT

Place of origin US

Date of origin 1990s

Breed registries GCCF, TICA

Weight range 12–22lb (5.5–10kg)

Grooming

Colors and patterns
Brown mackerel tabby only.

A breed developed in the 1990s by crossing a striped, shorthaired cat with a Bengal (pp.94–95), the Toyger has a tiger-marked coat with random vertical stripes that are quite distinct from any other tabby pattern. Well built and muscular, this unique "toy tiger" moves with the flowing power and grace of a big jungle cat. The Toyger is confident and outgoing but has a relaxed attitude to life, which allows it to fit in well with any household. Although active and athletic, this cat is easy to handle and can be taught to play games and to walk on a lead.

Long, broad head

Short, lush, glittery coat

Round eyes have deep color

Small, rounded ears are thickly furred

Kitten

Butterfly markings on head

Long, strong body carried low to the ground

Well-muscled neck

Powerful forequarters

Long, muscular, low-set, ring-marked tail

Brown mackerel tabby coat

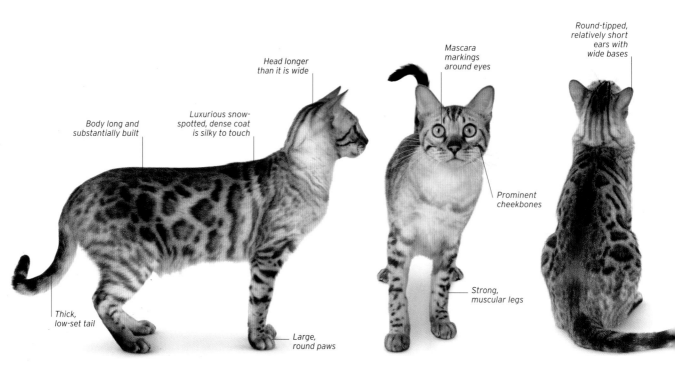

Head longer than it is wide

Luxurious snow-spotted, dense coat is silky to touch

Body long and substantially built

Thick, low-set tail

Large, round paws

Mascara markings around eyes

Prominent cheekbones

Strong, muscular legs

Round-tipped, relatively short ears with wide bases

BENGAL

THIS CAT HAS A STRIKINGLY BEAUTIFUL SPOTTED COAT AND A VIBRANT PERSONALITY

Place of origin US

Date of origin 1970s

Breed registries FIFe, GCCF, TICA

Weight range 12-22 lb (5.5-10 kg)

Grooming

Colors and patterns
Brown, blue, silver, and snow colors in spotted, marble classic, or lynx (tabby) pointed patterns.

In the 1970s, scientists crossed the small, wild Asian leopard cat with shorthaired domestic cats in an attempt to introduce the wild cat's natural immunity to feline leukemia into the pet population. The project failed, but the resulting hybrid caught the interest of several American fanciers. In a series of selective breeding programs, crosses were achieved between these hybrids and various pedigree domestic cats, including the Abyssinian (p.83), Bombay (p.36), British Shorthair (pp.68-77), and Egyptian Mau (p.80). The outcome was the Bengal, originally called the Leopardette, which was officially accepted as a new breed in the 1980s.

With its magnificently patterned coat and large, muscular frame, this cat brings more than a hint of the jungle into the living room. Despite its wild ancestry, there is nothing unsafe about the Bengal—it is delightfully affectionate—but it does have a lot of energy and is best suited to

an experienced cat owner. Friendly by nature, a Bengal always wants to be at the heart of its family and needs company and both physical activity and mental stimulation. A bored Bengal will be unhappy and possibly destructive.

SNOW MARBLE CLASSIC TABBY

The Bengal's soft, short coat may be either a spotted or dramatic swirling marble pattern (as shown here). A snow-colored coat usually indicates Burmese or Siamese ancestry.

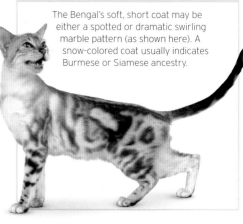

KANAANI

THIS RARE BREED LOOKS LIKE A WILD DESERT CAT BUT HAS AN AFFECTIONATE NATURE

Place of origin Israel

Date of origin 2000s

Breed registries Other

Weight range 11–20lb (5–9kg)

Grooming

Colors and patterns
Spotted and marbled tabby patterns with various ground colors.

Developed to have a close resemblance to the spotted African wildcat, the Kanaani is rare and many authorities do not yet accept it as a breed. Until 2010 the breeding program for this cat allowed crosses with the African wildcat, Bengal (pp.94–95) and Oriental Shorthair (pp.43–51)—provided all these had spotted coats. Since then, kittens must have Kanaani parents only. With its big, slender body, long legs, and long neck, the Kanaani stands out as an unusual breed. This cat has a gentle and affectionate temperament but at the same time retains some of the independence of its wild ancestor and is also an excellent hunter.

Large, almond-shaped green eyes

Long, slender, muscular body

Spots softened by ticking

Characteristic "M" marking on forehead

Brick-red nose leather

Long, slim, muscular legs

Black-tipped tail has at least three black rings

Kitten

Large ears with tufted tips

Broad, triangular-shaped head

Long neck

Compact, oval paws

Short, coarse-textured, seal-spotted tabby coat

SAVANNAH

THIS TALL, GRACEFUL CAT HAS A STRIKINGLY UNUSUAL APPEARANCE

Place of origin US

Date of origin 1980s

Breed registries TICA

Weight range 12–22lb (5.5–10kg)

Grooming

Colors and patterns
Brown spotted tabby, black silver-spotted tabby, black, or black smoke. Ghost-spotting may be visible in black or black smoke.

One of the newest cat breeds, the Savannah was officially recognized only in 2012. It originated from the chance mating of a male serval, a wild cat of the African plains, with a domestic female cat. The Savannah has inherited many of the serval's physical characteristics—including a spotted coat, long legs, and huge, upright ears—but is perhaps best known for its personality. This adventurous and athletic cat is permanently on the lookout for amusement, which might include playing with water, exploring the contents of a cupboard, or opening doors. Since a Savannah can be quite demanding, the breed is not best suited to first-time cat owners.

Brow slightly hooded

Long neck

Long, slender, athletic body

Parallel stripe markings run from top of head along length of body

Extremely large, upright ears set high on head

Triangular head small in proportion to body

Brown-spotted tabby coat lies flat and has slightly coarse texture, though spots feel softer

Very long, muscular legs

Smaller spots on legs and paws

SERENGETI

TALL AND ELEGANT, THIS BREED HAS A GENTLE BUT OUTGOING TEMPERAMENT

Place of origin	US
Date of origin	1990s
Breed registries	TICA
Weight range	8-15 lb (3.5-7 kg)
Grooming	

Colors and patterns
Black solid color; spotted tabby in any shade of brown or silver (silver ground color with black spots); and black smoke.

Designer-bred to resemble the serval—a small, leggy wild cat of the African grasslands—the Serengeti was created in California in the mid-1990s and is now also known in Europe and Australia. The result of crossing a Bengal (pp.94-95) with an Oriental (pp.43-51), this breed stands out among others with its long neck and legs and upright stance. Most conspicuous are the Serengeti's exceptionally large ears, which are the same length as its head. This agile cat enjoys climbing and exploring high places. It bonds closely with its owner and is an ideal companion for someone who spends a lot of time at home.

Large, round eyes

Well-rounded whisker pads

Long, lean, athletic body

Fine, dense silver spotted tabby coat

Head longer than broad

Exceptionally large, wide-based ears with rounded tips

Distinct, widely spaced spots

Long neck in proportion to body

Very long legs

Dark tail tip

CHAUSIE

THIS SLENDER, SLINKY CAT HAS A CHARISMATIC AIR

Place of origin	US
Date of origin	1990s
Breed registries	TICA
Weight range	12–22 lb (5.5–10 kg)

Grooming

Colors and patterns
Black solid and ticked tabby pattern in brown and grizzled black.

Although the wild jungle cat and the domestic cat could, and probably did, interbreed naturally in the past, the Chausie originated from hybrids created during the 1990s. Initially, the jungle cat was crossed with a variety of cats, but today, to maintain consistency of the Chausie's shape and coat color, only the Abyssinian (p.83) and certain domestic shorthairs are used. Like other hybrid cats, the Chausie is very active and enjoys exploring. It is intelligent and insatiably curious—a Chausie quickly becomes adept at opening doors to pry into cupboards. This cat requires an experienced owner who is able to spend plenty of time at home to provide companionship.

Eyes inclined to outer edge of ear

Long, high cheekbones

Ears have rounded tips

Round paws small in proportion to cat's size

Long head with sloping profile

Tall ears positioned on top of head and fairly close together

Large, lean, well-muscled body

Brown-ticked coat

Full whisker pads on muzzle

End of tail has tabby barring and dark tip

Long legs with faint barring on outer sides

MUNCHKIN

FRIENDLY AND SWEET, THIS SHORT-LEGGED CAT IS HIGHLY SOCIABLE

Place of origin	US
Date of origin	1980s
Breed registries	TICA
Weight range	6–9 lb (2.5–4 kg)
Grooming	

Colors and patterns
All colors, shades, and patterns.

The first Munchkins were bred in Louisiana, and although they are now achieving some popularity in both shorthaired and longhaired versions (p.181), they are not accepted by many international breed organizations. The exceptionally short legs of the Munchkin, which arose as a random mutation, do not appear to affect speed of movement or longevity. This little cat may not have the jumping ability of its taller cousins, but it still manages to climb on furniture and is lively and playful. The Munchkin has been used to create other short-legged breeds such as the Minskin.

Flat forehead

High, well-defined cheekbones

Round paws

Broad-based ears set on top of head

Black coat with white markings

Rounded, wedge-shaped head

Slight nose stop

Fairly dense, weather-resistant lilac coat

Tail as long as body

Well-rounded chest

Legs about half the average length of other breeds

KINKALOW

THIS NEW AND RARE BREED IS SAID TO BE INTELLIGENT AND PLAYFUL

Place of origin	US
Date of origin	1990s
Breed registries	TICA
Weight range	6–9lb (2.5–4kg)

Grooming

Colors and patterns
Many colors and patterns, including tabby and tortoiseshell.

A designer dwarf cat, the Kinkalow was deliberately created in the 1990s by crossing the Munchkin (p.101) with the American Curl (p.109). This still experimental breed ideally should have the small, compact body and ultra-short legs of the Munchkin combined with the turned-back ears of the Curl. Not all Kinkalow litters inherit these extreme traits, however, which are due to genetic mutations, and some kittens are born with both normal-length legs and straight ears. The development of the Kinkalow and the establishment of its breed standard are ongoing projects. So far, this miniature cat appears to be free from specific health problems and unhampered by its short legs.

Pink nose leather

Soft, sleek black coat

Curled-back ears inherited from American Curl

Silky red and black tortie coat

Short, compact body feels heavy for size

Tail long in comparison with body

White chest

Forelegs particularly short

SKOOKUM

DESPITE BEING ONE OF THE SMALLEST OF ALL BREEDS, THIS CAT IS FULL OF CONFIDENCE

Place of origin	US
Date of origin	1990s
Breed registries	Other
Weight range	6–9lb (2.5–4kg)

Grooming

Colors and patterns
All colors and patterns.

As a cross between the Munchkin (p.101) and the LaPerm (p.123), this little cat has inherited two striking features: extremely short legs and a soft coat, either long or short, that stands away from its body in exuberant curls or waves. The curly coat is not generally prone to matting and is easy to groom. The Skookum has been developed in several countries, initially in the US, and also in the UK, Australia, and New Zealand. However, it is still rare and has not yet achieved universal recognition. This is an active, playful cat, able to run and jump just as well as longer-legged breeds.

Ears very wide at base

Walnut-shaped eyes look large for head

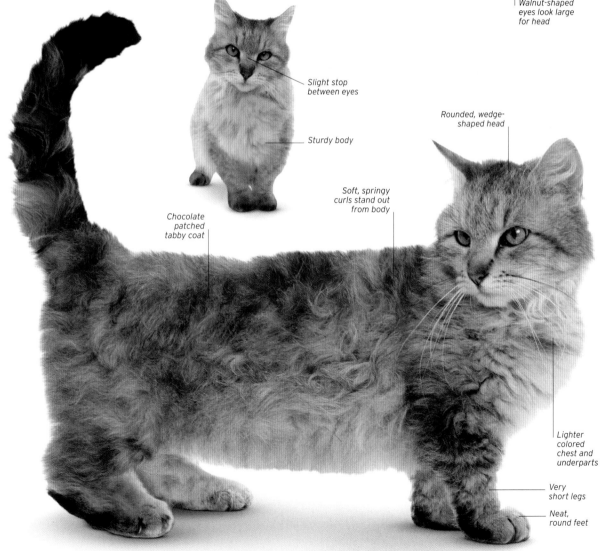

Slight stop between eyes

Sturdy body

Rounded, wedge-shaped head

Soft, springy curls stand out from body

Chocolate patched tabby coat

Lighter colored chest and underparts

Very short legs

Neat, round feet

LAMBKIN DWARF

THIS SWEET AND EASY-TO-KEEP CAT IS ACTIVE DESPITE HAVING VERY SHORT LEGS

Place of origin	US
Date of origin	1980s
Breed registries	TICA
Weight range	5–9lb (2–4kg)
Grooming	

Colors and patterns
All colors, shades, and patterns.

This little-known hybrid dwarf cat is a cross between the short-legged Munchkin (p.101) and the curly coated Selkirk Rex (pp.124–125). It is sometimes known as the Nanus (meaning dwarf) Rex. The Lambkin Dwarf is rare because it is extremely difficult to breed to type. In a single litter, some kittens may inherit both the mutant genes that pass on the short stature of one parent and the curly coat of the other, while other kittens may be short-legged and straight-haired, long-legged and straight-haired, or long-legged and curly-haired. These cats are reputed to have the docility of the Rex with a touch of the Munchkin's impishness.

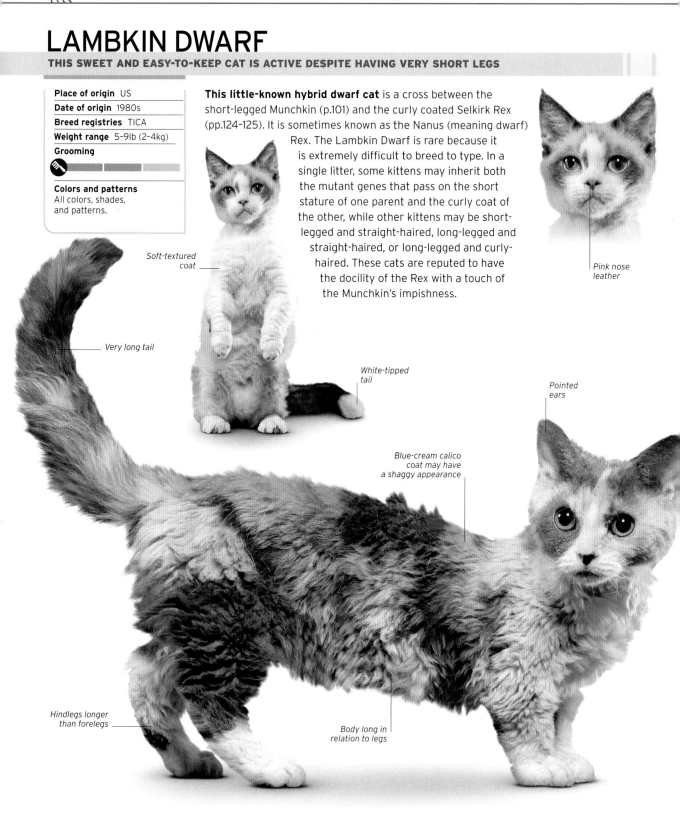

Soft-textured coat

Pink nose leather

Very long tail

White-tipped tail

Pointed ears

Blue-cream calico coat may have a shaggy appearance

Hindlegs longer than forelegs

Body long in relation to legs

BAMBINO

AN AMUSING COMPANION WITH AN AFFECTIONATE, KITTENISH PERSONALITY

Large, round eyes

Place of origin	US
Date of origin	2000s
Breed registries	TICA
Weight range	5–9lb (2–4kg)

Grooming

Colors and patterns
All colors, shades, and patterns.

This 21st-century experimental dwarf breed is one of the most extraordinary of all designer cats. Developed as a hybrid of the Munchkin (p.101) and the hairless Sphynx (pp.118–119), the Bambino is extremely short-legged with a heavily wrinkled skin that looks entirely naked, although it is usually covered with very fine peach-fuzz hair. Despite its dainty appearance, this cat is strong and athletic, with firm muscles and a sturdy bone structure. However, the lack of fur means that the Bambino is vulnerable to strong sun and low temperatures, and must be kept as an indoor pet. Grooming should consist of regular bathing to prevent a buildup of natural skin oils.

Strong neck

Very large, broad-based ears

Pronounced wrinkles on head

Short, firmly muscled legs

Wedge-shaped head

Well-rounded belly

Brittle whiskers are broken

Short, very fine downy hair has suedelike texture

Tapering, whiplike tail

Oval paws with long, slim toes

Unique ears
fold downward
and forward

Large, round
golden eyes

Short,
broad, slightly
curved nose

Short, dense blue
coat stands away
from body

Short
neck

Round, well-
padded body

Neat, round paws

Fairly long tail tapers
to rounded tip

SCOTTISH FOLD
A QUIET AND COMPANIONABLE CAT WITH UNIQUE FOLDED EARS

Place of origin	UK/US
Date of origin	1960s
Breed registries	CFA, TICA
Weight range	6-13 lb (2.5-6 kg)
Grooming	

Colors and patterns
Most colors, shades, and patterns, including pointed, tabby, and tortoiseshell.

Due to a rare genetic mutation, the ears of this breed fold forward to fit like a cap over the skull, producing a unique round-headed look. The first Fold cat to be discovered was an all-white, long-haired female, known as Susie, that was born on a Scottish farm in the 1960s. At first, this cat and the folded-ear kittens she produced attracted only local interest, but then geneticists began taking notice, and some of Susie's descendants were sent to the US. Here, the breed was established, using crosses between Folds and British (pp.68-77) and American Shorthairs (p.61). During the development of the Scottish Fold, a long-coated version (p.183) also emerged.

These cats need careful breeding to avoid certain skeletal problems linked to the gene responsible for ear folding, and due to this risk, they do not meet with the approval of all breed authorities. Scottish Folds are always born with straight ears that, in kittens carrying the folded-ear gene, begin to flatten forward within about three weeks. Cats that remain straight-eared are known as Scottish Straights (see box). The Scottish Fold is still something of a rarity, more likely to be seen at shows than as a house cat. However, the breed is known for its loyal nature, and Scottish Folds that do become pets adjust easily to any type of family, making quiet and affectionate companions.

SCOTTISH STRAIGHT

Apart from having upright ears, the Scottish Straight looks the same as the Fold. Straights are barred from shows, but it is hoped that they will soon be recognized as a separate breed.

HIGHLANDER

THIS ACTIVE AND PLAYFUL CAT PROVIDES PLENTY OF FAMILY ENTERTAINMENT

Place of origin	North America
Date of origin	2000s
Breed registries	TICA
Weight range	10–25 lb (4.5–11 kg)

Grooming

Colors and patterns
All colors in any tabby pattern, including colorpoints.

This recently developed breed, which also comes in a longhaired version (p.186), is still extremely rare. It has distinctive looks, with a big body, short tail, and dense coat. Most noticeable of all are the Highlander's large, curled ears; often thickly tufted, they add to the cat's air of wildness. Although not yet popular, the breed is beginning to earn recognition as a delightful house cat with a very special personality. Highlanders are ready to love everyone and make devoted companions. They have an irrepressible sense of fun, always want to play, and are said to be easy to train.

Wide muzzle

Well-defined whisker pads

Spots merge into stripes along top of back

Distinctive ears curl back loosely at tips, no more than 90 degrees

Large eyes set wide apart

Large, round paws

Broad, well-muscled shoulders

Short, thick tail

Broad nose

Brown-spotted tabby coat

AMERICAN CURL

AN ELEGANT AND ENGAGING CAT THAT MAKES A LOVING COMPANION

Place of origin US

Date of origin 1980s

Breed registries CFA, FIFe, TICA

Weight range 7–11 lb (3–5 kg)

Grooming

Colors and patterns
All colors, shades, and patterns.

The first American Curls were longhaired (pp.184–185) like the founding female of the breed, which was discovered in California. The shorthaired version was developed later and is essentially the same cat in a different coat. Big-eyed and elegantly proportioned, the American Curl is extremely attractive to look at. The curled ears, which may appear within a week of birth, add a touch of designer chic, although the mutation is an entirely natural phenomenon. This breed, noted for its sweet temperament, forms a close attachment to its family and always wants to know what is going on in the household.

Wedge-shaped head

Prominent whisker pads

Short, silky, brown-spotted tabby coat lies flat to body

Ears turn smoothly back at least 90 degrees

Large, brilliant eyes

Rectangular, moderately muscled body

Flexible, broad-based tail

Rounded paws

JAPANESE BOBTAIL

A CHARMING CAT WITH A BEAUTIFUL VOICE AND A UNIQUE POM-POM TAIL

Place of origin Japan	
Date of origin c.17th century	
Breed registries CFA, FIFe, TICA	
Weight range 6–9lb (2.5–4kg)	
Grooming	

Colors and patterns
All colors and patterns, including tabby (except ticked), tortoiseshell, and bicolor.

In its native Japan this cat is said to bring good luck and is a popular subject for ceramic figurines. The Japanese Bobtail was spotted in the 1960s by an American enthusiast, who sent a number of the cats to the US to begin a breeding program. This shorthaired version won recognition in the late 1970s, followed a decade or so later by the longhaired version (p.188). An attractive and beautifully proportioned cat, the Japanese Bobtail is outgoing and intelligent. It has a charmingly melodious voice and fond owners like to claim that it talks, or even sings, to them.

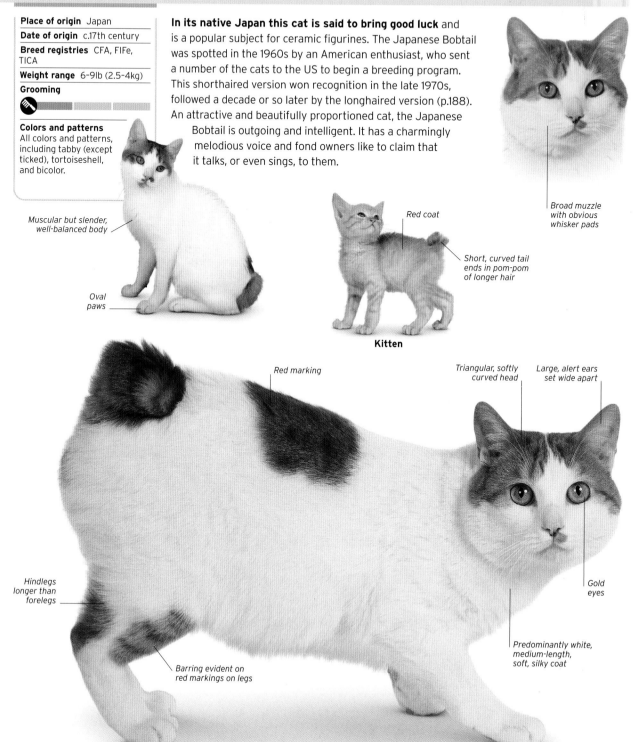

Broad muzzle with obvious whisker pads

Muscular but slender, well-balanced body

Oval paws

Red coat

Short, curved tail ends in pom-pom of longer hair

Kitten

Red marking

Triangular, softly curved head

Large, alert ears set wide apart

Gold eyes

Predominantly white, medium-length, soft, silky coat

Hindlegs longer than forelegs

Barring evident on red markings on legs

KURILIAN BOBTAIL

THIS STURDY AND STRONG-LIMBED CAT HAS A QUIRKY TAIL

Place of origin Kuril Islands, North Pacific

Date of origin 20th century

Breed registries FIFe, TICA

Weight range 7–10lb (3–4.5kg)

Grooming

Colors and patterns
Most solid colors and shades in bicolor, tortoiseshell, and tabby (except ticked) patterns.

Native to the Kuril Islands, which form a chain between the North Pacific and the Sea of Okhotsk, off Siberia, the Kurilian Bobtail first became popular as a domestic cat in mainland Russia during the 20th century. Since the 1990s this breed, in longhaired (p.189) as well as shorthaired versions, has also been appearing regularly at Russian cat shows but it is little known elsewhere. The curious tail is a natural mutation and differs from one cat to another; it always has a number of kinks and may curl or bend in almost any direction. Kurilian Bobtails are relaxed, sociable cats, and said to be superb mousers.

Slightly angled, large eyes

Broad, straight nose

Short, kinked tail at least two vertebrae long

Triangular ears tilt slightly forward

Close-lying brown mackerel tabby coat has minimal undercoat

Well-muscled, compact body

Broad, slightly rounded chin

Strong legs with solid bone structure

Well-developed thighs

MEKONG BOBTAIL

THIS LITTLE-KNOWN BREED HAS AN ATTRACTIVE SIAMESE-POINTED COAT

Place of origin Southeast Asia

Date of origin Pre-20th century

Breed registries Other

Weight range 8–13 lb (3.5–6 kg)

Grooming

Colors and patterns
Colorpoints as Siamese (pp.54–57).

Named after the great Mekong River that flows through China, Laos, Cambodia, and Vietnam, this short-tailed cat occurs naturally over a wide area of Southeast Asia. The Mekong Bobtail was developed as an experimental breed in Russia and has been recognized by some authorities since 2004, although worldwide it is not particularly well known. It is a strongly built cat with the brilliant blue eyes and colorpointed coat of a Siamese. The Mekong Bobtail is active and agile and is good at jumping and climbing. It is said to be a quiet breed with a friendly, well-balanced personality.

Prominent cheekbones

Short, glossy coat with minimal undercoat

Medium, broad-based ears

Large, almond-shaped, bright blue eyes

Solidly built, medium-size, rectangular body

Short, kinked tail

Legs slender in comparison to body

Hindlegs longer than forelegs

Cream coat with chocolate pointing

Oval paws

AMERICAN BOBTAIL

BIG AND BEAUTIFUL, THIS CAT IS AN EXCELLENT AND HIGHLY ADAPTABLE COMPANION

Place of origin	US
Date of origin	1960s
Breed registries	CFA, TICA
Weight range	7–15 lb (3–7 kg)

Grooming

Colors and patterns
All colors, shades, and patterns, including tabby, tortoiseshell, and colorpoint.

The breeding of domestic bobtail cats native to the US has been reported several times since about the middle of the 20th century, but so far only this one has been fully recognized. There is also a longer-haired version (p.193), and both types have the naturally occurring shortened tail that gives the breed its name. The American Bobtail is a substantially built cat, with powerful muscles and large bones. It is intelligent, alert, and reasonably active but also enjoys quiet times. This cat is happy to be among people, without overwhelming them with its attention, and fits in comfortably with any type of household.

Broad, wedge-shaped head

Muzzle slightly wider than long

Semi-dense, medium-short coat has soft undercoat

Large whisker pads

Tufted ears with slightly rounded tips

Distinctive heavy brow

Nose wide with large leather

Moderately long, powerful body

Broad-based tail with seal pointing

Deep flanks

Tabby markings on legs

Large, round paws

TAIL TYPES
Manx cats are classified according to tail length. Categories include "rumpy" (completely tailless); "stumpy" (the tail has from one to three vertebrae); and "longy" (the tail is almost normal length).

MANX

BEST KNOWN OF THE TAILLESS CATS, THIS BREED IS POPULAR FOR ITS QUIET CHARM

Place of origin	UK
Date of origin	Pre-18th century
Breed registries	CFA, FIFe, GCCF, TICA
Weight range	8–12 lb (3.5–5.5 kg)

Grooming

Colors and patterns
All colors, shades, and patterns, including tabby and tortoiseshell.

Few breeds have as many stories about their origins as the tailless Manx. Among the more nonsensical legends, this cat is supposed to have lost its tail in an accident on Noah's Ark. In reality, it is native to the Isle of Man, in the Irish Sea, and its lack of tail is a natural mutation. The Manx has interested cat fanciers since the early 20th century and, together with its long-haired relation, the Cymric (p.192), is known worldwide. Breeding is carefully controlled to avoid the spinal problems sometimes associated with tailless cats. The Manx is gentle and calm and can be trained to play "fetch" or walk on a lead.

Calico coat

Red classic tabby coat has clearly delineated texture

White paws

Rump has characteristic rounded appearance

Eyes angled slightly toward nose

Round head with full cheeks

Short tail stump

Large whisker pads

Heavily muscled hindlegs much longer than forelegs

Sturdy, compact body with deep flanks

Heavily boned legs

Kitten

PIXIEBOB

HEFTY AND MUSCULAR, THIS CAT LOOKS FIERCE BUT HAS A SWEET TEMPERAMENT

Place of origin	US
Date of origin	1980s
Breed registries	TICA
Weight range	9–18lb (4–8kg)
Grooming	

Colors and patterns
Brown spotted tabby only.

Like the mountain bobcat from which it derives its name, the Pixiebob has a thick coat, tufted ears, a pointed face, and a powerful body, and moves with loose-limbed grace. A common feature of this breed—which, unusually, is accepted in the breed standard—is the occurrence of extra toes (polydactylism) on one or more paws. Both the Pixiebob shorthair and a longhaired variant (pp.190-1) have richly colored, spotted coats that complete the illusion of a wild cat. Despite appearances, the Pixiebob is entirely domestic in character, loves family life, clings to its owners, plays with children, and good-naturedly accepts other pets.

Thickly furred above eyes

Brick-red nose leather

Short coat has woolly texture and stands away from body

Brown spotted tabby coat

Deep flanks

Well-muscled body

Short bob tail

Broad chest

Lighter color on underparts, throat, and chest

Long, heavily boned legs

Long, broad paws

AMERICAN RINGTAIL

A WELL-BUILT AND PLUSH-COATED CAT WITH A TWIST IN ITS TAIL

Place of origin US
Date of origin 1990s
Breed registries TICA
Weight range 7–15lb (3–7kg)
Grooming

Colors and patterns
All colors, shades,
and patterns.

No other cat possesses this breed's unique tail, which is carried in a flexible curl over the back or flank. The American Ringtail was discovered by chance in California and, so far, its development has included the introduction of Oriental-type lines. These cats are still few and far between, but interest among breeders is gradually increasing. There is also a longhaired version. Ringtails love games, climbing, and nosing around anything that appeals to their strong sense of curiosity. The soft trilling sounds that they make gave them their original name of Ringtail Sing-a-Ling.

Large almond-shaped eyes

Soft, dense brown classic tabby coat with plush texture

Flexible tail carried in a ring over back

Long body with athletic build

Broad, wedge-shaped head

Ears deeply cupped

Powerful hindquarters

Medium-length, square muzzle

Hindlegs slightly longer than forelegs

White markings on chest and chin

Large, oval white paws

LYKOI

A LITHE, INTELLIGENT, AND OUTGOING CAT WITH A UNIQUE ROAN FUR

Place of origin	US
Date of origin	2011
Breed registries	CFA, GCCF, TICA
Weight range	7–15 lb (3–7 kg)

Grooming

Colors and patterns
Black roan.

This new breed, established only in 2011, has been likened to a werewolf due to its unique appearance. The Lykoi displays a rare, naturally occurring mutation that affects its fur, leaving it partially hairless. First observed in the US in feral cats, the Lykoi was developed by outcrossing to black shorthaired cats that carried the recessive form of the mutated gene and to feral cats that possessed the same unique coat. A black shorthaired cat carrying the Lykoi gene was brought to the UK in 2013, where, two years later, the first Lykoi kitten was born. There are now both long- and shorthaired varieties of the Lykoi in the UK.

Large, oval, amber eyes

Muzzle with rounded, hairless whisker pads

Evenly distributed white guard hairs make the fur roan

Tapering tail shorter than body

Large ears with wide bases set high on head

Fur unevenly distributed over the body

Medium-sized, oval feet

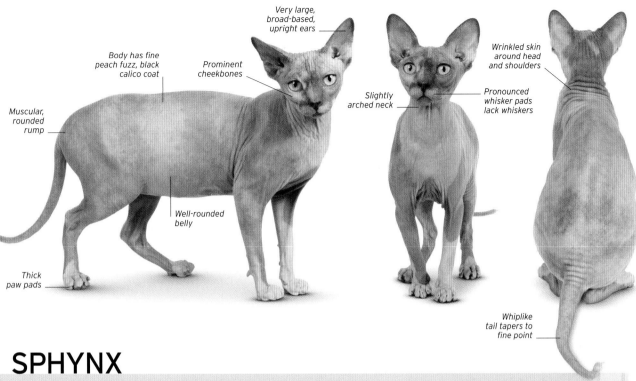

Very large, broad-based, upright ears

Body has fine peach fuzz, black calico coat

Prominent cheekbones

Slightly arched neck

Wrinkled skin around head and shoulders

Pronounced whisker pads lack whiskers

Muscular, rounded rump

Well-rounded belly

Thick paw pads

Whiplike tail tapers to fine point

SPHYNX

THIS HAIRLESS CAT HAS AN ENDEARINGLY IMPISH CHARACTER

Place of origin Canada

Date of origin 1960s

Breed registries CFA, FIFe, GCCF, TICA

Weight range 8–15 lb (3.5–7 kg)

Grooming

Colors and patterns
All colors, shades, and patterns.

Probably the best known of the hairless cats that have appeared around the world, the Sphynx originated in Canada and was named for its supposed resemblance to the Ancient Egyptian sculpture of the mythical Sphinx. The cat's hairlessness is a natural mutation, and interest in its development dates from the birth of a hairless male kitten produced by a short-coated farm cat in Ontario in 1966. This kitten, along with other hairless kittens that appeared over the following decade, was used to found the breed.

Although hairlessness is commonly accompanied by other mutations, careful selective breeding, including outcrosses to Devon Rex (pp.128–129) and Cornish Rex (pp.126–127) cats, has ensured that the Sphynx is relatively free of genetic problems. Sphynx cats are not completely bald—most have a coating of fine, suedelike fuzz on their bodies and often a little thin hair on their head, tail, and paws. Undeniably an extraordinary-looking cat—with its enormous

ears, wrinkled skin, and rounded belly—the Sphynx does not appeal to everyone, but its delightfully sociable and loving nature has created more than a few converts. It is easy to live with but needs to be kept indoors and protected from temperature extremes. Lack of a normal coat also means that excess body oils cannot be absorbed, so regular washing is required. Cats used to baths from an early age are unlikely to object.

WRINKLY SKIN

The Sphynx's wrinkled skin is not unique to the breed—all cats are the same under their fur. Sphynx kittens are wrinkly all over; adults have wrinkles mainly on the shoulders and head.

DONSKOY

A CAT WITH OTHERWORLDLY LOOKS BUT A LOVABLE NATURE

Place of origin Russia
Date of origin 1980s
Breed registries FIFe, TICA
Weight range 8–15 lb (3.5–7 kg)
Grooming

Colors and patterns
All colors, shades, and patterns.

The founder of this breed (also known as the Don Sphynx) was an ill-treated kitten rescued from the streets in the Russian city of Rostov-on-Don. This stray lost its apparently normal coat as it matured and produced offspring with the same mutation. Various coat types occur in the Donskoy—some individuals are truly hairless, while others have a partial coat that can be fuzzy or even wavy. Uniquely, the hairless types may develop temporary fur patches in winter. With wrinkled skin and oversized ears, the Donskoy does not have universal appeal, but aficionados praise its gentleness, sparkling personality, and social ease. Grooming consists of regular bathing to remove excess oil from the skin.

Folds on forehead

Arched, powerful neck

Very large, open ears are set wide apart and tilt slightly forward

Elastic, heavily wrinkled skin

Green eyes slant upward

Coat type varies from hairless to wiry or wavy

Muscular, strongly boned body

Broad chest

Long, whippy tail

Thick, cushionlike paw pads

Very long, webbed toes

PETERBALD

AN ELEGANT, GRACEFUL BREED WITH A VARIETY OF COAT TYPES

Place of origin	Russia
Date of origin	1990s
Breed registries	FIFe, TICA
Weight range	8–15 lb (3.5–7 kg)

Grooming

Colors and patterns
All colors, shades, and patterns.

Originating in Russia, the Peterbald is a fairly new breed created by crossing the Oriental Shorthair (pp.43–51) with the Donskoy (left). This cat is highly variable and may be completely hairless; covered with a fine soft down; or possess a dense, stiff coat with a brushlike texture. Kittens born with a coat may become hairless as they mature, sometimes retaining downy-coated points. The Peterbald has a pleasant temperament and makes a good family cat. Hairless or very thin-coated varieties need protection from the elements and are probably best kept indoors. The skin of hairless types may have a sticky feel and needs regular bathing.

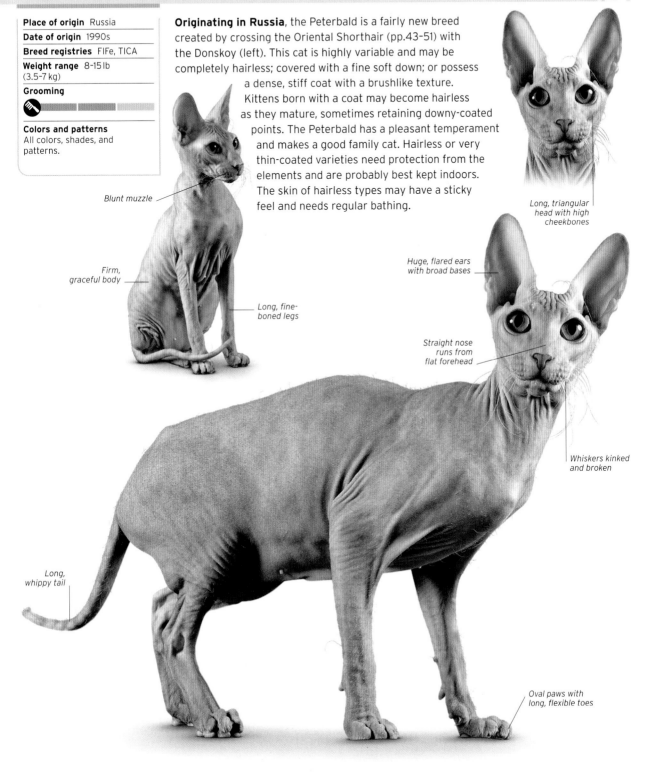

Blunt muzzle

Firm, graceful body

Long, fine-boned legs

Long, triangular head with high cheekbones

Huge, flared ears with broad bases

Straight nose runs from flat forehead

Whiskers kinked and broken

Long, whippy tail

Oval paws with long, flexible toes

URAL REX

THIS UNUSUAL-LOOKING REX BREED IS NOT YET WIDELY KNOWN

Place of origin	Russia
Date of origin	1980s
Breed registries	Other
Weight range	8–15lb (3.5–7kg)

Grooming

Colors and patterns
Various colors and patterns, including tabby.

The first of these wavy-coated cats was born near Yekaterinburg, a major Russian city set in the foothills of the Ural Mountains. Carefully developed over three decades, the Ural Rex is very popular among cat fanciers in Russia and is also now being bred in Germany. This breed's fine, dense, double coat may be short or semi-long; the distinctive, close-lying waves, which have an elastic quality, can take up to two years to develop fully. Grooming is not difficult but must be carried out regularly. The Ural Rex is described as a quiet and good-natured cat that makes an excellent household companion.

Upright ears set high on head

Prominent cheekbones

Large, oval eyes set wide apart

Slim, muscular, relatively short body

Broad, flat forehead

Short, wedge-shaped head

Fine, silky black-smoke coat lies close to body in loose curls

White chest, underparts, and legs

Medium-length, moderately thin tail

Slender legs with small paws

LAPERM

A BRIGHT AND INQUISITIVE CAT WITH A KITTENISH ENERGY THAT LASTS INTO ADULTHOOD

Place of origin US

Date of origin 1980s

Breed registries CFA, FiFe, GCCF, TICA

Weight range 8–12lb (3.5–5.5kg)

Grooming

Colors and patterns
All colors, shades, and patterns, including colorpoint.

This rex-coated breed originated on a farm in Oregon and was later developed into both shorthaired and longhaired (pp.196–7) versions. The LaPerm has a highly strokable coat that may be either wavy or curly and has a light, springy texture. Outgoing and not shy about asking for attention, this cat makes a loving and lively pet. LaPerms adapt themselves easily to homes of all types and become deeply attached to their owners. They need company and should not be left alone for too long. Gentle combing or the occasional shampoo and towel dry are recommended as the best ways of maintaining the coat.

Large, expressive gold eyes

Very long, wavy whiskers

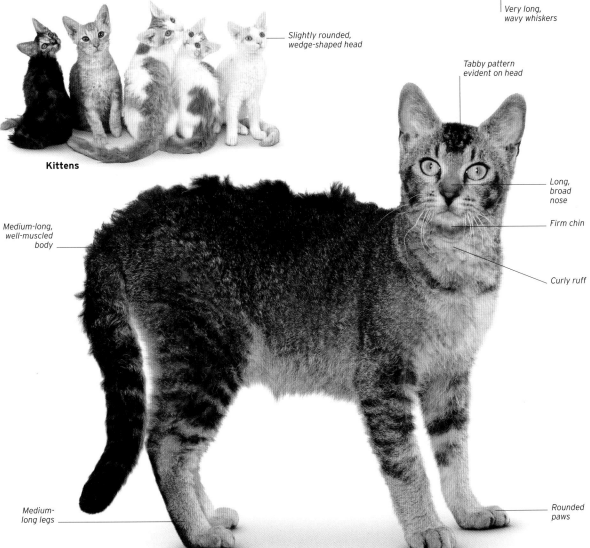

Slightly rounded, wedge-shaped head

Kittens

Tabby pattern evident on head

Long, broad nose

Firm chin

Curly ruff

Medium-long, well-muscled body

Medium-long legs

Rounded paws

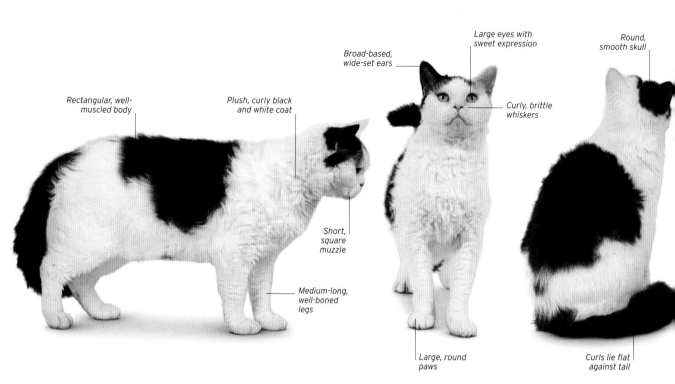

Rectangular, well-muscled body

Plush, curly black and white coat

Broad-based, wide-set ears

Large eyes with sweet expression

Round, smooth skull

Curly, brittle whiskers

Short, square muzzle

Medium-long, well-boned legs

Large, round paws

Curls lie flat against tail

SELKIRK REX

A HAPPY TEDDY BEAR OF A CAT THAT ENJOYS A LOT OF COMPANY

Place of origin	US
Date of origin	1980s
Breed registries	CFA, FIFe, GCCF, TICA
Weight range	7–11lb (3–5kg)
Grooming	

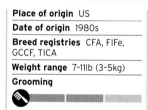

Colors and patterns
All colors, shades, and patterns.

This cat takes its name from the Selkirk Mountains near its place of origin in Montana. Created in the late 1980s, the breed had its beginnings in an animal rescue center, where a curly coated kitten appeared among an otherwise straight-coated litter born to a feral cat. This kitten became the founding female of the Selkirk Rex. As the breed was developed, planned matings with pedigree cats produced both the Selkirk Rex shorthair and a longer-coated type (p.194) that was the result of crosses with Persians. Straight-coated variants are common in litters of both types.

The dense, soft coat of the Selkirk Rex falls into random curls or waves, rather than in the neat lines sometimes seen in other rex breeds. A greater degree of curl often occurs around the neck and belly. The whiskers are sparse and curly, and tend to snap off easily.

Grooming a Selkirk Rex is not difficult but a light touch is advisable, because overly vigorous brushing can flatten out the curls.

Though calm and tolerant, this cat is far from staid and loves a hug. Selkirks stay kittenish for years and always enjoy games.

GOING CURLY

The curls of a Selkirk Rex can take up to two years to develop fully. Kittens are born with curly coats that usually straighten out for a few months before starting to turn curly again when the cat is about eight months old.

GROWING A FULL COAT
All Cornish Rex kittens are born with wavy coats, but some of them lose this for a few weeks and have a temporary, suedelike covering. By three months, the waves should be nearly fully formed.

CORNISH REX

THIS ATHLETIC CAT HAS CURLS FROM WHISKERS TO TAIL

Place of origin UK

Date of origin 1950s

Breed registries CFA, FIFe, GCCF, TICA

Weight range 6–9 lb (2.5–4 kg)

Grooming

Colors and patterns
All solid and shaded colors and patterns, including tabby, tortoiseshell, colorpoint, and bicolor.

The founder of this svelte breed was a wavy-coated male cat born in a Cornish farmhouse. Descendants of this original sire were crossed with other breeds—including the Siamese (pp.54–57), Russian Blue (p.66), and American (p.61) and British Shorthairs (pp.68–77)— improving the stamina and genetic diversity of the Cornish Rex and adding a wide variety of colors. With its super-fine, rippled coat and streamlined body, this cat stands out from all the rest. It is an extrovert with a large repertoire of amusing antics and a kittenish outlook on life, but it turns into an affectionate lap cat when play is over. Because of its thin coat, this breed is vulnerable to temperature extremes and should be groomed with a light touch. In the US, it has developed differently and has a more wedge-shaped head.

Large, oval eyes are set wide apart

High, chiseled cheekbones

Slim, elongated, well-muscled body

Outer ear is hairless

Fairly small, wedge-shaped head

Short, fine, white coat forms tight, uniform waves

Straight nose

Finely boned, long, slender legs

Small, oval paws

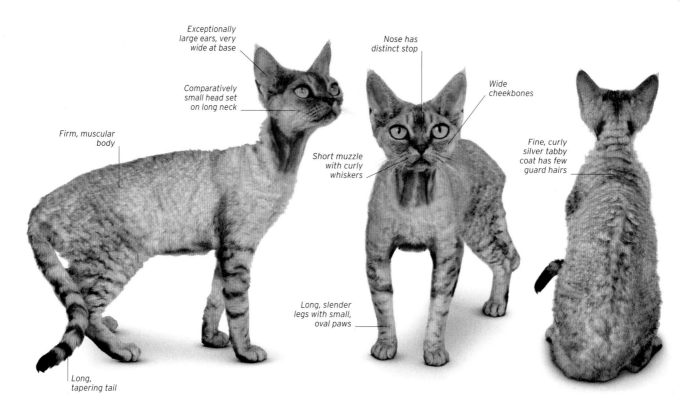

Exceptionally large ears, very wide at base

Comparatively small head set on long neck

Firm, muscular body

Nose has distinct stop

Wide cheekbones

Short muzzle with curly whiskers

Fine, curly silver tabby coat has few guard hairs

Long, slender legs with small, oval paws

Long, tapering tail

DEVON REX

NICKNAMED THE PIXIE CAT, THIS MISCHIEVOUS BREED HAS AN ABUNDANCE OF ENERGY

Place of origin	UK
Date of origin	1960s
Breed registries	CFA, FIFe, GCCF, TICA
Weight range	6–9 lb (2.5–4 kg)

Grooming

Colors and patterns
All colors, shades, and patterns.

A curly coated feral tom and an adopted stray tortoiseshell were the founders of this highly specialized breed, which originated in Buckfastleigh, Devon, UK. A litter produced by this unlikely pair included a curly coated kitten, which was used in the first program to develop the breed. To begin with, it was assumed that this new Devonian line could be crossed with the Cornish Rex (p.127), another wavy-coated breed discovered a short distance away and a few years earlier. When only normal-coated kittens resulted from the matings, it was realized that two different recessive genes, arising in surprisingly close geographical proximity, had produced slightly different rexed coats.

The coat of the Devon Rex is fine and very short, with few guard hairs. Ideally, the waves should be loose and distributed evenly over the body, but the degree of wave or curl varies from cat to cat and may alter with seasonal shedding of hair or as a cat matures. The whiskers are crinkly and tend to be brittle, breaking off before reaching full length. Because of their thin coats, these cats can seem warmer to the touch than most breeds, but they easily become chilled and need a draft-proof accommodation. A Devon Rex's coat usually needs little more than a wipe-down to keep it in good condition; these cats will also tolerate gentle bathing, provided they are introduced to water when they are young kittens.

Despite its slender, leggy appearance, the Devon Rex is far from fragile and possesses boundless energy for playing games and scaling heights. This cat adores attention and is not suitable for a family that will be away from the home all day.

GERMAN REX

A CAT THAT NEEDS PLENTY OF QUALITY TIME WITH ITS HUMAN FAMILY

Place of origin	Germany
Date of origin	1940s
Breed registries	FIFe
Weight range	6–10 lb (2.5–4.5 kg)

Grooming

Colors and patterns
All colors, shades, and patterns.

A feral cat adopted in Berlin just after the end of World War II was the founding female of this breed. As the German Rex was developed, cats were imported to other parts of Europe and to the US. The wavy coat of this cat arises through the same mutant gene that appears in the Cornish Rex (p.127), which for some years was included in German Rex breeding programs; in some countries, the two breeds are not recognized as separate. A good-natured and friendly cat, the German Rex will play with anyone but also likes quiet times staying close to its owners. Because the short coat does not absorb natural oils efficiently, regular bathing is necessary.

Brilliant blue eyes

Short, curly whiskers

Short, wavy coat with velvety texture

Rounded paws

Kittens

Broad-based ears

Round head with well-defined cheekbones

Cream coat shaded with sepia in places

Medium-length, strongly built body

Strong, rounded chest

Sepia pointing on tail, legs, and face

Medium-length, moderately fine legs

AMERICAN WIREHAIR

THIS VERSATILE, FRIENDLY CAT IS HAPPY INDOORS OR OUTDOORS AND WITH FAMILIES OF ALL AGES

Place of origin	US
Date of origin	1960s
Breed registries	CFA, TICA
Weight range	8–15 lb (3.5–7 kg)

Grooming

Colors and patterns
Variety of solid colors and shades in various patterns, including bicolor, tabby, and tortoiseshell.

In New York in 1966, a wire-haired kitten appeared in a litter born to two domestic cats with normal coats. This was the founder of the American Wirehair breed, which was later developed by using American Shorthairs (p.61). The genetic mutation that produced the distinctive coat is not known to have occurred anywhere outside the US. In a Wirehair, each hair is crimped and bends over or forms a hook at the end, resulting in a coarse, springy texture that has been likened to steel wool. In some cats, the coat can be brittle, so grooming—preferably by bathing—should be gentle to avoid damage.

Large, round, copper-colored eyes

Curly whiskers

Prominent cheekbones

Dense, springy brown classic tabby and white coat with crimped hairs and coarse texture

Medium-size ears with rounded tips

Medium to large, well-muscled body

Back level from shoulders to rump

Rounded rump

Medium-boned, muscular legs

Firm, rounded paws

HOUSE CAT–SHORTHAIR

THESE HARDY CATS MAKE EXCELLENT, EASY-TO-KEEP PETS

The first domestic cats had short coats, and the type still predominates wherever in the world cats are kept as house pets. Random-bred shorthairs occur in nearly every possible color permutation, with tabbies, torties, and traditional solid colors being the most common. The majority of these cats are solidly in the middle range when it comes to body shape. Selective breeding, which has created some extreme lines, has largely bypassed the shorthaired house cat, although occasionally a hint of, for example, the lean Oriental shape suggests an out-of-the-ordinary parentage.

Typical tabby "M" marking on forehead

RED CLASSIC TABBY AND WHITE
Large size and a dense coat could point to British or American Shorthair in the history of this handsome cat. However, his green eyes may be part of a different inheritance.

BLUE AND WHITE
In house cats, white markings are rarely as symmetrical as those considered desirable in pedigrees. However, a solid color splashed with white is always striking, and a random effect adds individual charm.

Irregularly spaced ring markings on tail

BROWN TABBY
The broken stripes on this cat are, in fact, intermediate between mackerel and spotted tabby patterns. Tabby markings often occur in domestic cats and show up well on short coats.

Mixture of colors

CALICO
Tortoiseshell, or tortie, patterning occurs in many color forms, black and red being the traditional combination. A calico, tortie with white areas over more than half its body, is known as a tortie and white cat in the UK.

BLUE MACKEREL TABBY AND WHITE
While tabbies with white markings are very common, the blue variation would be a lucky find in a random-bred cat. This one's markings are indistinct against the background color.

RAGDOLL
One of the largest pedigree cats, the semi-longhaired Ragdoll was developed in the 1960s. This spectacular breed comes in several dramatic patterns, all with bright blue eyes.

LONGHAIRS

It is thought that long hair in domestic cats arose as a genetic mutation. In cooler climates this trait would be advantageous and so its frequency in the cat population probably increased, and was later selected for by cat breeders. Wild cats have thicker rather than longer coats and have no role in the ancestry of domestic longhairs.

The curly coated Selkirk Rex longhair is an unusual variation

Types of longhair

The first longhaired cats seen in Western Europe arrived some time in the 16th century. These were the Angoras, a slender, silky-coated Turkish breed that enjoyed a certain popularity until they were usurped by a new type of longhair, the Persian, in the 19th century. Sturdier than the Angoras, Persians had longer, thicker fur, immense tails, and round faces. By the end of the 19th century they were the longhair of choice for cat lovers. The Angora vanished, not to be seen again until the breed was re-created by enthusiasts in the 1960s (p.159).

The Persian remains a steady favorite, but since the 20th century other longhairs have been attracting attention. These include cats described as semi-longhaired, which have medium-long coats but a less dense, fluffy undercoat than the Persian. One of the most magnificent of the semi-longhairs is the Maine Coon, native to North America. Huge and handsome, this breed has a shaggy look due to the variable length of the hair in its topcoat. Almost equally striking is the big blue-eyed Ragdoll, while the brush-tailed Somali has the graceful lines of the Abyssinian cat from which it was developed. More in the style of the original Angoras is the beautiful Balinese—a semi-longhair version of the Siamese—which has silky, flowing, close-lying fur.

Striving for yet more variety, breeders have crossed longhairs with some of the more unusual shorthairs. Bobtails, curled-ear and folded-ear breeds, the wavy-coated Selkirk Rex, and the LaPerm with its fleecelike curly fur are all now found with luxuriantly long coats.

Grooming longhairs

Many longhaired cats shed their coats heavily, especially in the warmer seasons, when they can have a much sleeker appearance. Frequent grooming—a daily session may be needed in some breeds—keeps loose hairs to a minimum and prevents the thick undercoat from matting.

MAINE COON
This American breed was once an outdoor farm cat. Its naturally thick coat gave protection in bitter New England winters.

PERSIAN
For more than a hundred years the extravagantly coated Persian has been the most popular longhair.

Short nose with break between eyes

Full cheeks

Large head with broad skull

Small, rounded ears with long tufts

Orange-colored eyes

Body sturdy and deep-chested

Long, thick, fine-textured white coat

Short, sturdy legs

Deep ruff

Short tail

PERSIAN—SOLID

THIS CHARMING CAT IS THE ORIGINAL VERSION OF THE WORLD'S FAVORITE LONGHAIR

Place of origin	UK
Date of origin	1800s
Breed registries	CFA, FIFe, GCCF, TICA
Weight range	8–15 lb (3.5–7 kg)

Grooming

Colors and patterns
Black, white, blue, red, cream, chocolate, and lilac.

By the end of the 19th century, when pedigree cat shows were starting to attract worldwide interest, the Persian (sometimes referred to as the Longhair) was already very popular in the US and the UK. This luxuriously coated cat came to the show benches after a long but obscure history in Europe, and it is not known whether the true ancestors of the breed did, in fact, originate in Persia (Iran). The first recognized Persians were solid-colored—that is, they had coats of one solid color.

The earliest known examples of the breed were pure white, often with blue eyes—a color combination commonly associated with deafness unless breeding is carefully managed. Cross-breeding with solid Persians in other colors produced orange eyes, and white Persians with orange, blue, or different-colored eyes (one of each color) became accepted. Queen Victoria can be given credit for making blue Persians popular—they were her favorite cats—and

black and red were other early solid colors. Since about the 1920s onward, further solid-colored varieties have been developed, including cream, chocolate, and lilac.

Characteristically, a Persian has a round head with a flat face; snub nose; and large, round, appealing eyes. The body is compact and sturdily built, and the legs are short and strong. The magnificently thick, long coat is a major commitment for the owner of a Persian. Daily grooming is a must to prevent the fur from tangling or developing impenetrable mats that are hard to remove.

Persians are renowned for their gentle, affectionate temperament and home-loving personality. These are definitely not action cats, although they can be charmingly playful if offered a toy.

The flattened features of the Persian, overemphasized in modern breeding programs, have led to health issues. Breathing difficulties and problems with the tear ducts are common in this cat.

PERSIAN–BLUE- AND ODD-EYED BICOLOR
THESE UNCOMMON PERSIANS ARE HARD TO FIND, BUT THEIR POPULARITY IS ON THE RISE

Place of origin UK

Date of origin 1900s

Breed registries CFA, FIFe, GCCF, TICA

Weight range 8–15 lb (3.5–7 kg)

Grooming

Colors and patterns
White with various solid colors, including black, red, blue, cream, chocolate, and lilac.

Accepted in the cat fancy world only since the late 1990s, the Blue- and Odd-eyed Bicolor and Tricolor are variations of the Persian Bicolor (p.154). The Odd-eyed is less common than the Blue-eyed, although its enchantingly different look is increasing in popularity. In this cat, one eye is blue and the other copper, with both eyes equally brilliant in color. The mismatch is difficult to produce, since mating between two odd-eyed cats does not guarantee a litter of odd-eyed kittens.

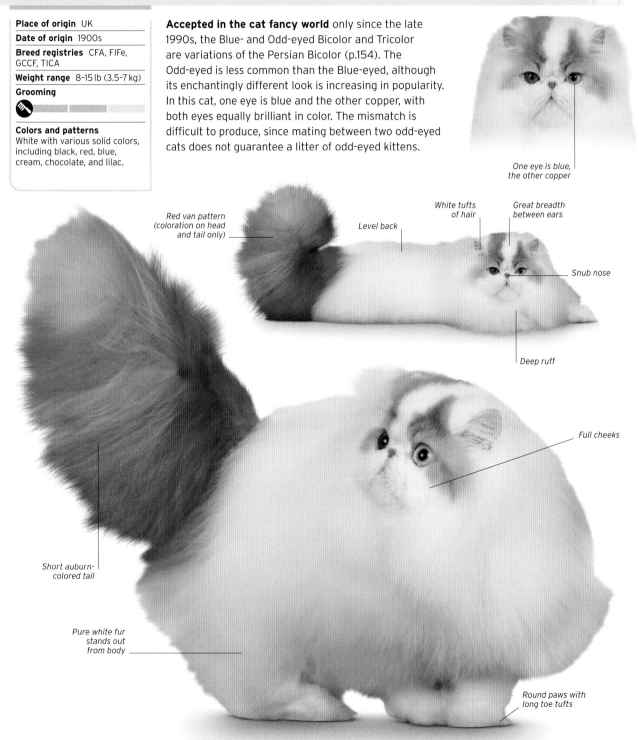

One eye is blue, the other copper

Red van pattern (coloration on head and tail only)

Level back

White tufts of hair

Great breadth between ears

Snub nose

Deep ruff

Short auburn-colored tail

Full cheeks

Pure white fur stands out from body

Round paws with long toe tufts

PERSIAN—CAMEO

THIS BREED HAS SOFTLY BLENDED COLORS IN A RIPPLING COAT

Place of origin US, Australia, and New Zealand

Date of origin 1950s

Breed registries CFA, FIFe, GCCF, TICA

Weight range 8–15 lb (3.5–7 kg)

Grooming

Colors and patterns
Red, cream, black, blue, lilac, and chocolate solid colors and tortoiseshell patterns.

Regarded by many cat fanciers as the most glamorous of all the Persian colors, this version was developed in the 1950s by crossing Smoke (p.148) and Tortoiseshell (p.152) longhairs. The fur of a Cameo is white with color, most often a shade of red, carried at the ends of the hair shafts to varying degrees. In the "tipped" variety, the color appears only at the very tip of each hair but extends to up to a third of the hair shaft in "shaded" cats. Cameo gives the effect, especially as the cat moves, of changing hues.

Deep copper eyes

Pink nose leather

Cream shaded cameo coat

Shading on legs

Pale inner ear tufts

Darker markings on face

Main area of color on back and flanks

Ears set toward side of head

Underside of plumed tail lighter in color

Paler fur on chest and underparts

Hair shorter on lower legs

PERSIAN–CHINCHILLA

THIS SILVERY-COATED BREED HAS MOVIE-STAR LOOKS

Place of origin UK

Date of origin 1880s

Breed registries CFA, FIFe, GCCF, TICA

Weight range 8–15 lb (3.5–7 kg)

Grooming

Colors and patterns
White, tipped with black.

The first Chinchilla appeared in the 1880s, but it was the James Bond series of films, starting in the 1960s, that brought this cat fame when it was seen on screen as the pet of the super-spy's archenemy, Blofeld. Chinchillas have a shimmering, silvery-white coat in which each hair is tipped with black. The breed's name derives from the likeness of its coat coloration to that of a small South American rodent called the chinchilla, once a victim of the fashion trade for its beautiful, soft fur.

Black lining around eyes, nose, and lips

Red nose leather

Silvery sparkle to coat

Blue-green eyes

Long white tufts of hair

Black tipping evenly distributed over white coat

Pure white on chest and belly

Shorter coat on lower legs

PERSIAN–GOLDEN

ONCE REGARDED AS THE WRONG COLOR, THIS CAT IS NOW A MUCH-PRIZED PET

Place of origin UK

Date of origin 1920s

Breed registries CFA, FIFe, GCCF, TICA

Weight range 8–15 lb (3.5–7 kg)

Grooming

Colors and patterns
Apricot to golden with seal-brown or black tipping.

Recognized as a new breed in the US since the 1970s, this cat has a gloriously colored coat of rich apricot to golden fur that is widely admired. Yet the first Golden Persians, which appeared in the 1920s in litters born to Chinchillas (opposite), were regarded as rejects as far as the pedigree cat world was concerned. They were known generally as brownies, and, though barred from the show bench, made appealing pets. Later, breeders saw the potential of Goldens and worked to develop this lovely Persian variation.

Blue-green eyes

Rose-pink nose leather

Eyes, lips, and nose rimmed with black

Domed head

Kitten

Thick ruff around neck

Lightest coloring on chest and belly

Long pale apricot tufts of hair

Golden coat with rich coloring on back

Paler underside to tail

Darker coloration on legs due to seal-brown tipping

PERSIAN–PEWTER

THIS STRIKING, COPPER-EYED CAT HAS AN ATTRACTIVELY TIPPED COAT

Place of origin	UK
Date of origin	1900s
Breed registries	CFA, FIFe, GCCF, TICA
Weight range	8–15 lb (3.5–7 kg)

Grooming

Colors and patterns
Very pale with black or blue tipping.

Years of careful breeding, at first using crosses with Persian Chinchillas (p.140), produced the two current variations of Pewter. These cats, originally referred to as Blue Chinchillas, have pale, almost white, coats with blue- or black-tipped hair. This coloration gives the effect of a mantle extending from the top of the head and down the back. Pewter kittens are born with traditional tabby markings, which gradually fade in intensity but are still retained to some degree in adult cats. The very special look of this breed is enhanced by its characteristic deep orange to copper-colored eyes.

Nose break between eyes

Dark-rimmed, copper-colored eyes

Ghost tabby "M" marking on forehead

Very pale chest

Darkest tipping on back and flanks

Black pewter coat

Dark tip to tail

Faint tabby markings on legs

Face lightly tipped only

PERSIAN–CAMEO BICOLOR

THIS LOVELY BREED IS TRULY A PERSIAN OF MANY COLORS

Place of origin US, New Zealand, and Australia

Date of origin 1950s

Breed registries CFA, FIFe, GCCF, TICA

Weight range 8–15 lb (3.5–7 kg)

Grooming

Colors and patterns
Red, cream, blue-cream, black, blue, lilac, and chocolate colors with white; calico pattern.

The color combinations of this version of the Cameo (p.139) are almost endless. As well as the shading and tipping that characterize the Cameo coat, in which the hair shafts are colored only partway along their length, the addition of both bicolor and tricolor patterns make this breed seem like many different cats. Shades of red are common, but black, blue, chocolate, cream, and tortoiseshell (black and red, or blue and cream) also appear, all with extensive areas of white. The contrast between the patches of sparkling white and color of varying intensity is stunning.

Pink nose leather

Deep copper eyes

Darker markings on face

Ears set toward side of head

Pale tufts of hair

Short, rounded body

Main area of red shading on back and flanks

Underside of tail lighter in color

Majority of coat is white

PERSIAN—SHADED SILVER
AN EXQUISITELY COLORED CAT WITH LUMINOUS BLUE-GREEN EYES

Place of origin UK

Date of origin 1800s

Breed registries CFA, FIFe, GCCF, TICA

Weight range 8–15 lb (3.5–7 kg)

Grooming

Colors and patterns
White with black tipping.

This Persian bears some resemblance to the Chinchilla (p.140), both breeds having white coats tipped on the ends of the hairs with a darker color. At one time, these cats were described as silvers. However, over decades of development from the 20th century onward, Chinchillas have become paler and the Shaded Silver can now usually be distinguished by having the darker coloring of the two. In particular, breeders of Shaded Silvers strive to achieve the characteristic dark mantle that falls over the back.

Blue-green eyes

Eyes, nose, and lips are black-rimmed

Silver shaded coat

Rose-pink nose leather

White fur on chin and chest

White underside to tail

Mantle of black tipping, darkest on back, flanks, and tail

Well-developed nose stop

Short, sturdy legs

PERSIAN–SILVER TABBY

THIS CAT IS A SILKY, SILVERY-COATED VERSION OF THE TRADITIONAL TABBY

Place of origin UK

Date of origin 1800s

Breed registries CFA, FIFe, GCCF, TICA

Weight range 8–15 lb (3.5–7 kg)

Grooming

Colors and patterns
Silver tabby; patched silver tabby; all with white patches.

Some of the most delicately colored Persians of all are the Silver Tabbies. These cats have well-defined tabby coat patterns, but the warm coppery ground colors of the traditional tabby are replaced by a silvery- or bluish-white undercoat. Bicolor Silver Tabby cats have clear white areas, preferably as a minimum on the muzzle, chest, underparts, and sometimes legs. In the Tricolors, a further color—such as a shade of red or brown—is blended into the coat.

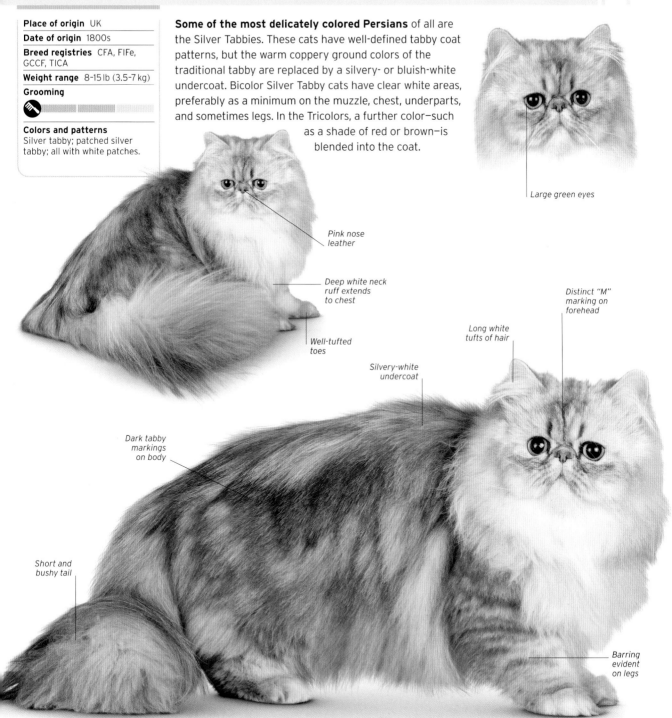

Large green eyes

Pink nose leather

Deep white neck ruff extends to chest

Well-tufted toes

Distinct "M" marking on forehead

Long white tufts of hair

Silvery-white undercoat

Dark tabby markings on body

Short and bushy tail

Barring evident on legs

PERSIAN—SMOKE
THIS RARE-COLORED BREED HAS BEEN SAVED FROM THE BRINK OF EXTINCTION

Place of origin UK

Date of origin 1860s

Breed registries CFA, FIFe, GCCF, TICA

Weight range 8–15 lb (3.5–7 kg)

Grooming

Colors and patterns
White deeply tipped with color, including black, blue, cream, and red, and in tortoiseshell patterns.

In the coat patterning of the Smoke, each hair is pale at the base, becoming darker by degrees along its length. Smoke kittens are born without any apparent sign of this coloring, which does not start developing until the cat is several months old. Smoke Persians were recorded as early as the 1860s, but they have never been common. By the 1940s, this breed had all but disappeared. Fortunately, a few enthusiasts continued to develop the Smoke, creating new interest in the breed and extending its range of colors.

Dark blue mask and ears

Black nose leather

Full white frill on black smoke coat

Typical cobby Persian body

Legs are solid color

Short, bushy tail

White undercoat, more apparent in motion

Blue smoke coat

Ears set far apart

Lighter underparts

PERSIAN–SMOKE BICOLOR

BEAUTIFULLY BLENDED COLORS MAKE THIS CAT ONE OF THE PRETTIEST PERSIANS

Place of origin UK

Date of origin 1900s

Breed registries CFA, FIFe, GCCF, FICA

Weight range 8–15 lb (3.5–7 kg)

Grooming

Colors and patterns
White with smoke colors, including blue, black, red, chocolate, lilac, and various tortoiseshells.

This multi-hued breed has a coat combining areas of white with various smoke colors, in which each hair is colored for most of its length but is white at the base. Smoke produces greater depth of color than in shaded or tipped coats, and the pale base may not be apparent until the cat moves. Bicolored Smoke Persians can have areas of black, blue, chocolate, lilac, and red smoke with white, while the Tricolors include several tortoiseshell smokes, such as blue and cream tortie.

Extensive color patches on head

Black nose leather

White muzzle

Heavily plumed tail

White tufts of hair

Brilliant copper eyes

Softly blended blue smoke coat

Deep chest with pure white ruff

Long guard hairs

PERSIAN—TABBY AND PATCHED TABBY

THIS GENTLE CAT HAS BEEN BRED IN A RICH VARIETY OF COLORS AND PATTERNS

Place of origin UK

Date of origin 1800s

Breed registries CFA, FIFe, GCCF, TICA

Weight range 8–15 lb (3.5–7 kg)

Grooming

Colors and patterns
Many colors also with silver tipping in tabby and patched-tabby patterns.

The tabbies have a longer history than many of the other Persians. Brown tabbies appeared in some of the earliest cat shows in the UK in the 1870s, and one of the first purebred cat fancy clubs was established to promote the breed. Since those days, the Persian Tabby has been developed in several colors, and three pattern types are accepted: classic (or blotched), mackerel (with narrow streaks), and spotted. In Patched Tabbies (sometimes known as tortie tabbies), the tabby markings overlay a bicolored ground coat.

Red nose leather

Black line runs from corner of eye

Round copper-colored eyes

Nose has sharp break between eyes

Brown classic tabby coat

Barring on legs

Dense black markings on body

Tabby "M" mark on forehead

Full, brushlike tail

Short, sturdy legs with large, round paws

Necklace markings on upper chest

PERSIAN–TABBY BICOLOR
A BREED WITH RICH TABBY COLORING HIGHLIGHTED BY WHITE PATCHES

Place of origin UK

Date of origin Post 1900

Breed registries CFA, FIFE, GCCF, TICA

Weight range 8–15 lb (3.5–7 kg)

Grooming

Colors and patterns
Classic and mackerel tabby pattern, in various colors with white.

This lovely variation of the Persian combines sparkling white with the warm colors of the tabby. Two types of markings are accepted: classic tabby (sometimes called blotched tabby), in which the markings appear as large, smudged areas; and mackerel tabby, which is marked with thinner dark streaks or stripes. Tabby Bicolor and Tricolor Persians were first given championship status in the 1980s, and their beautiful markings, softly blurred by the lush coat, have made them strong favorites with cat breeders and owners.

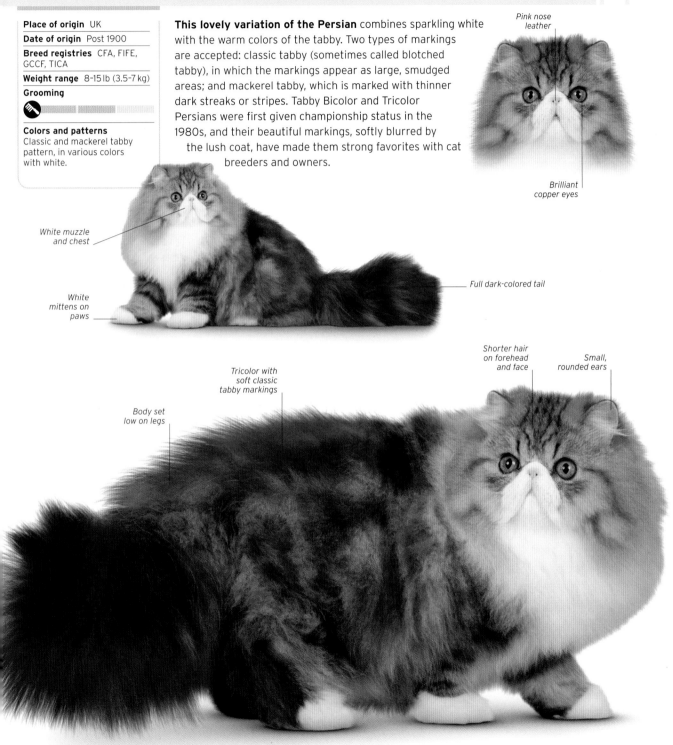

Pink nose leather

Brilliant copper eyes

White muzzle and chest

White mittens on paws

Full dark-colored tail

Shorter hair on forehead and face

Small, rounded ears

Tricolor with soft classic tabby markings

Body set low on legs

PERSIAN–TORTIE AND CALICO

THESE PERSIANS WITH POPULAR COLORS ARE NOT ALWAYS EASY TO OBTAIN

Place of origin UK

Date of origin 1880s

Breed registries CFA, FIFe, GCCF, TICA

Weight range 8–15 lb (3.5–7 kg)

Grooming

Colors and patterns
Tortoiseshell (black and red), chocolate tortoiseshell, lilac-cream, and blue-cream; also with white patches.

Tortoiseshell cats—frequently called torties—have a coat that is a mixture of two colors, giving a mottled appearance. Persian Torties have been known since the late 19th century, but they have always been difficult to breed consistently. Their genetic make-up means that nearly all cats with tortie coloring are females and the few males that do occur are sterile. There is a tricolored version of this Persian, the Calico (known as Tortie and White in the UK).

Bright copper eyes

Black nose leather

Fine-textured, silky calico coat

Very short muzzle

Clear black and red patches on body

White chest and muzzle

White legs and paws

Several shades of red blend softly with black areas in tortie coat

Long tufts of red hair

Strong, thick legs

PAINTBOX PATTERN
A splash of red tabby added to black and white creates a vivid mix of colors. Calico (also known as tortie and white) is particularly dramatic when seen on the long, silky hair of a Persian.

PERSIAN—BICOLOR

A LONGHAIR WITH BOLD COLOR PATCHES FOR EXTRA GLAMOUR

Place of origin UK

Date of origin 1800s

Breed registries CFA, FIFe, GCCF, TICA

Weight range 8–15 lb (3.5–7 kg)

Grooming

Colors and patterns
White with various solid colors, including black, red, blue, cream, chocolate, and lilac, and with tortoiseshell patterns.

Up until the 1960s, bicolored Persians were of little interest to breeders and were considered suitable only as pets. Today, they are challenging the solid colors in popularity on the show benches. One of the first bicolors to be recognized was black and white, once referred to as magpie; now many other solid colors combined with white are accepted. In producing bicolor and calico cats, breeders aim for clearly defined, symmetrical markings—an ideal that is difficult to achieve.

Chocolate color on head

White muzzle

Color patches well defined and symmetrical

Long hair at base of ears

Black nose leather

Copper-colored eyes

Chocolate and white, fine-haired, silky coat

Chocolate-colored tail

White chest and underside

White legs and paws

HIMALAYAN

THIS CAT HAS SHOW-STOPPING LOOKS AND A PEACEFUL TEMPERAMENT

Place of origin US

Date of origin 1930s

Breed registries CFA, FIFe, GCCF, TICA

Weight range 8–15 lb (3.5–7 kg)

Grooming

Colors and patterns
Solid, colored, and tortie and lynx patterned points.

Known as the Persian–Colorpoint in the UK, the Himalayan is the result of more than a decade of breeding programs aimed at producing a longhair with Siamese markings. Round-faced and snub-nosed, with large eyes; a short, sturdy body; and long, lush fur, the Himalayan has all the typical Persian characteristics. It is a cat that loves to be loved, although as a companion it is quiet and undemanding. Daily grooming is a must for this breed, because the dense, double coat is inclined to mat without regular attention.

Round face with broad skull

Short, snub nose with pronounced stop between eyes

Face mask of contrasting seal color

Seal point coat

Broad, stocky body

Large, round paws with long tufts between toes

Long, thick ivory-colored coat over entire body

Large blue eyes

Small ears with rounded tips

Short, brushlike tail with seal pointing

Deep ruff

BALINESE

A VERY SPECIAL CAT THAT IS REFINED IN APPEARANCE BUT WITH HIDDEN STEEL

Place of origin US

Date of origin 1950s

Breed registries CFA, FIFe, GCCF, TICA

Weight range 6–11 lb (2.5–5 kg)

Grooming

Colors and patterns
Seal, chocolate, blue, and lilac solid colorpoints.

A longhaired version of the Siamese, the Balinese is an exquisite cat with the slender, graceful outlines of its relative draped in a flowing, silky coat. Records show that longhaired kittens have appeared occasionally among shorthaired Siamese litters for many decades, but it was not until the 1950s that some breeders began to develop the new look. The Balinese has an outgoing personality and is bursting with energy and curiosity. Although not as loud-voiced as the Siamese, it is attention-seeking, and also has a strong streak of mischief—owners of a Balinese would be well advised not to leave this cat to its own devices over long periods.

Clearly defined seal mask covers most of face

Long, straight nose with no break

Very large, wide-based ears

Almond-shaped deep blue eyes slant toward nose

Long, fine, close-lying lilac point coat

Seal point coat

Long, tapering, wedge-shaped head

Long, lithe, strong body

Plumed tail

Long, slender legs

Seal pointing on legs matches shading on body

BALINESE-JAVANESE

THIS CONFIDENT AND ATTENTION-SEEKING CAT DEMANDS A PLACE IN THE FAMILY

Place of origin US

Date of origin 1950s

Breed registries CFA

Weight range 6–11 lb (2.5–5 kg)

Grooming

Colors and patterns
Many point colors, in lynx and tortie patterns.

This enchanting cat is a development of the Balinese (opposite), the longhaired relation of the Siamese, with which it shares an identical breed standard in terms of conformation and coat quality. The difference between the two is the range of additional colors and patterns in the Javanese, which were acquired mostly through crosses with the Colorpoint Shorthair (p.58). Lithe and athletic despite its delicate appearance, the Javanese has a strong character to match. An affectionate, communicative cat, it loves to follow its owner around—when it is not prying into every nook and cranny of the house. The silky coat does not mat and is relatively easy to groom.

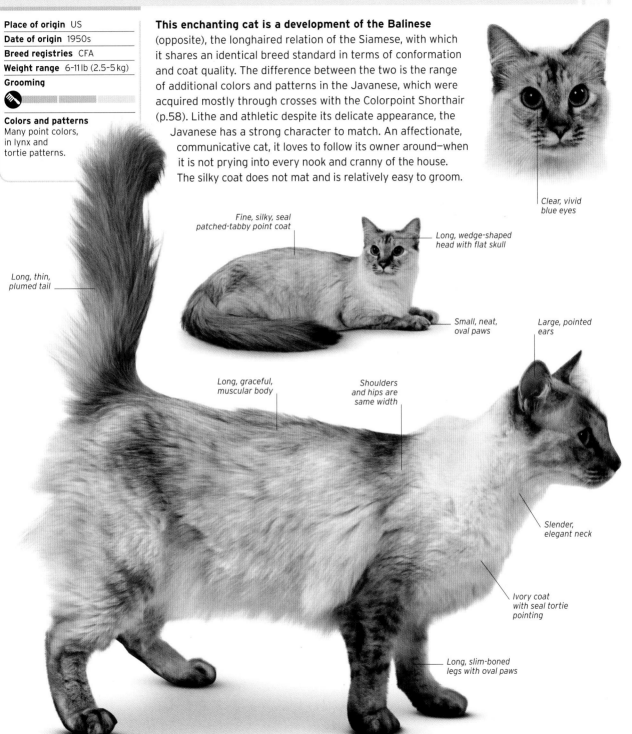

Clear, vivid
blue eyes

Fine, silky, seal
patched-tabby point coat

Long, wedge-shaped
head with flat skull

Long, thin,
plumed tail

Small, neat,
oval paws

Large, pointed
ears

Long, graceful,
muscular body

Shoulders
and hips are
same width

Slender,
elegant neck

Ivory coat
with seal tortie
pointing

Long, slim-boned
legs with oval paws

YORK CHOCOLATE

THIS BREED IS SWEET AND LOVING BUT AN AVID HUNTER OUTDOORS

Place of origin US

Date of origin 1980s

Breed registries Other

Weight range 6–11 lb (2.5–5 kg)

Grooming

Colors and patterns
Solid color: chocolate, lavender; bicolor: chocolate and white, lavender and white.

The founding female of the York Chocolate breed came from New York and was a dark chocolate brown, hence the breed's name. When kittens born to this cat had the same rich coloring, their owner developed an enthusiasm for continuing the line. Although still comparatively rare, the York Chocolate has attracted much attention at cat shows in North America. The breed includes bicolors with patches of chocolate or lavender. It is a gentle lap cat with an affectionate temperament and loves to be petted. In the home, this soft-voiced breed will quietly make its presence felt by following its owner everywhere and joining in with anything that is going on.

Large, pointed ears

Almond-shaped eyes

Medium-long muzzle

Semi-long, silky chocolate and white coat with thin undercoat

Plumed tail tapers to a point

Rounded head

Long, slender neck

Long, well-built but not heavy body

Paws tufted between toes

ORIENTAL LONGHAIR

A TYPICAL ORIENTAL CAT THAT NEEDS PLENTY OF COMPANY AND AMUSEMENT

Place of origin UK

Date of origin 1960s

Breed registries CFA, FIFe, GCCF, TICA

Weight range 6–11lb (2.5–5kg)

Grooming

Colors and patterns
Many colors, including solid, smoke, and shaded; tortie, tabby, and bicolor patterns.

Known originally as the British Angora, the Oriental Longhair was renamed in 2002 to avoid confusion with the Turkish Angora (p.178). The breed was developed in the 1960s in an attempt to recreate the silky-haired Angora cats that were favored pets in Victorian households until ousted by the up-and-coming Persians. Breeding programs included various longhaired Oriental cats, such as the Balinese (pp.156–157), producing what is in essence a longhaired Siamese—lithe-bodied and elegant but without colorpoints. Curious, playful, and highly active, the Oriental Longhair loves to be the center of family attention but often chooses one person with whom to form a close bond.

Striking, almond-shaped green eyes

Wide-based, triangular ears

Fine, silky, semi-long coat with no undercoat

Long, elegant neck

Rounded head

Chocolate coat color

Long, angular, well-muscled body

Plumed, tapering tail

Slender legs with fine bone structure

Neat, oval paws

TIFFANIE

THIS EASYGOING BREED MAKES AN IDEAL COMPANION FOR OWNERS OF ALL AGES

Place of origin UK

Date of origin 1980s

Breed registries GCCF, TICA

Weight range 8–14lb
(3.5–6.5kg)

Grooming

Colors and patterns
All solid and shaded colors;
tabby and tortie patterns.

Formerly called the Asian Longhair, and recognized as the Burmilla Longhair in US in 2015, the Tiffanie originated by chance as a longhaired variant of the Burmilla, a breed that itself originated as a happy accident following an unplanned mating between a European Burmese (p.39) and a Persian Chinchilla (p.140). The Tiffanie is a gentle, cuddly cat with a hint of mischief inherited from the Burmese side of its family. This cat is good at amusing itself with its own games, but is pleased if a human wants to join in. Sensitive and intelligent, the Tiffanie is said to be highly responsive to the moods of its owner.

*Yellow-green eyes
set well apart*

*Medium-long,
silky coat
darkens toward
base of tail*

*Broad, wedge-
shaped head*

*Fairly large,
wide-based ears*

*Thick ruff
around neck*

*Compact body
with straight,
muscular back*

*Blue-tipped
silver coat*

*Strong,
medium-
length legs*

*Long,
plumed tail*

Oval paws

CHANTILLY/TIFFANY

A RARE BREED WITH A SOFT, FULL, RICHLY COLORED COAT

Place of origin US

Date of origin 1960s

Breed registries Other

Weight range 6–11lb (2.5–5kg)

Grooming

Colors and patterns
Black, blue, lilac, chocolate, cinnamon, and fawn; various tabby patterns.

The history of the Chantilly/Tiffany starts with a litter of chocolate-brown kittens born to two longhaired cats of unknown origin. A once widespread belief that the Burmese was included in the breed's ancestry has now been discounted. The various names under which these cats have been registered during development of the breed—Foreign Longhair, Tiffany, and Chantilly—caused much confusion, and the dual name is now the most commonly accepted. Although very attractive and possessing a sweet personality, the Chantilly/Tiffany has not yet achieved great popularity. It loves human companionship but asks for it politely, attracting attention with a soft trill.

High cheekbones

Longer ruff around neck

Ears with rounded tips

Silky, semi-long chocolate coat has minimal undercoat

Almond-shaped eyes slightly angled

Nose slopes to broad muzzle

Legs strong but not heavy

Medium-long body

Long tail is thickly plumed

BIRMAN

THIS CAT IS QUIET AND GENTLE BUT HIGHLY RESPONSIVE TO AN OWNER'S ATTENTION

Place of origin Myanmar (Burma)/France

Date of origin c.1920s

Breed registries CFA, FIFe, GCCF, TICA

Weight range 6–9 lb (4.5–8 kg)

Grooming

Colors and patterns
All colorpoints, with white feet.

With its distinctive colorpoints, this exquisite cat has the appearance of a longhaired Siamese, but the two breeds are unlikely to be closely related. According to a charming legend, Birmans descend from the sacred white cats once kept by priests in Myanmar (Burma), their coloring bestowed by mysterious supernatural powers. In reality, the breed was probably created in France in the 1920s, though the foundation cats may have been acquired from Myanmar. Long-bodied and sturdily built, the Birman has silky textured hair that does not mat like that of many longhaired cats.

Full cheeks and round muzzle

Well-developed jaw

Round blue eyes

Silky blue point coat

Roman nose

Strong, elongated body

Thick ruff around neck

Paws have white gloves

Sturdy legs

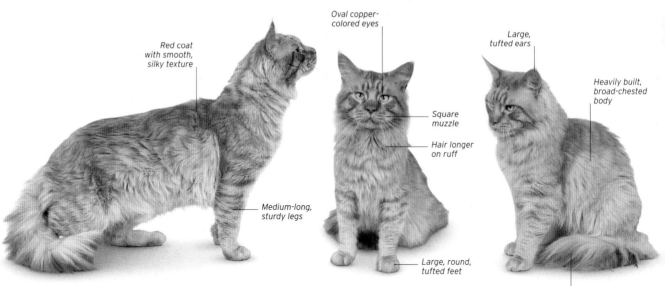

Red coat with smooth, silky texture

Oval copper-colored eyes

Large, tufted ears

Square muzzle

Heavily built, broad-chested body

Hair longer on ruff

Medium-long, sturdy legs

Large, round, tufted feet

Long, thick-furred tail

MAINE COON

AN IMPRESSIVELY LARGE CAT THAT IS KIND-NATURED AND EASY TO KEEP

Place of origin	US
Date of origin	1800s
Breed registries	CFA, FIFe, GCCF, TICA
Weight range	9–17 lb (4–7.5 kg)

Grooming

Colors and patterns
Many solid colors and shades in tortoiseshell, tabby, and bicolor patterns.

Regarded as America's native cat, the Maine Coon is named after the state where it was first recognized. How the breed first arrived there has been explained in various entertaining but mostly improbable tales. Wilder versions of the Maine Coon's history put forward the theory that it descends from Scandinavian cats brought in by the Vikings, or claim that several cats of this type were sent to the US by Marie Antoinette, anxious to preserve her pets during the French Revolution. The suggestion that the Maine Coon was originally a hybrid between feral cats and raccoons can definitely be discounted as a scientific impossibility, though the cat's bushy tail makes it easy to see how the idea might once have had credibility.

Huge and handsome, the Maine Coon has a thick, shaggy, waterproof coat that served it well in its earlier role as a farm cat, leading an outdoor life through harsh North American winters. Once highly regarded for its skills as a vermin catcher, this breed has become a popular pet since the mid-20th century. Maine Coons have many endearing characteristics, including a tendency to act like kittens all their lives. Their voice, described by some as a birdlike chirp, sounds surprisingly small for such a big cat. These cats are slow to mature and do not usually reach their full magnificent growth until about their fifth year.

SEASONAL COAT

A Maine Coon in full coat has an immense ruff, which is usually shaggier in males than in females. This provides excellent insulation and would have been a vital cold-weather accessory when Maine Coons were outdoor working cats. The coat changes seasonally, much of the thick undercoat being shed in summer.

WEATHERPROOF
The Maine Coon's massively thick coat keeps the cold out and warmth in. Even the long ear tufts are designed to protect the large, broad-based ears from the harshest weather.

RAGDOLL

THIS HUGE CAT IS REMARKABLY SWEET AND AMENABLE

Place of origin	US
Date of origin	1960s
Breed registries	CFA, FIFe, GCCF, TICA
Weight range	10-20 lb (4.5-9 kg)

Grooming

Colors and patterns
Most solid colors in tortie and lynx patterns; always pointed and bicolor or mitted.

The name is well chosen, because few cats are easier to handle or more ready to sit on a lap than a Ragdoll. One of the largest of all cat breeds, this cat has a confused history—supposedly, the original Ragdolls were developed from a litter of kittens born in California that became unusually limp and "floppy" when picked up. These cats love human company, will happily play with children, and are usually well disposed toward other pets. Ragdolls are not particularly athletic and, once past kittenhood, mostly prefer their games to be gentle. Moderate grooming is enough to keep their soft, silky fur free from tangles.

Large, oval, bright blue eyes

Kitten

Broad, wedge-shaped head

Wide-set ears

Seal bicolor coat becomes longer toward tail

Long, plumed tail

Very large, heavily boned body

Long, silky guard hairs cover woolly undercoat

Long feathering on hindlegs

Fur shorter on lower legs

RAGAMUFFIN

A MASSIVELY BUILT, BIG-HEARTED, AND DELIGHTFULLY CALM CAT

Place of origin	US
Date of origin	Late 20th century
Breed registries	CFA, GCCF
Weight range	10–20 lb (4.5–9 kg)

Grooming

Colors and patterns
All solid colors in bicolor, tortie, and tabby patterns.

This comparatively recent breed has a complicated history, but it emerged as a new development of the better-known Ragdoll (opposite). The RagaMuffin is a huge cat, a true gentle giant that fits in placidly with families of all types. It thrives on affection, and its docile temperament makes it an excellent pet for children. The RagaMuffin is not without a sense of fun and is easily persuaded to play with toys. This cat's dense, silky fur is not prone to matting, and short, regular grooming sessions will keep the coat in good order.

Dip in nose

Large eyes with characteristic sweet expression

Full cheeks

Long, plumed tail

Heavily built, rectangular body

Broad, rounded head

Wide-set ears with rounded tips

Thick, silky black and white coat does not mat easily

SOMALI

A CAT WITH DRAMATIC LOOKS, A GORGEOUS COAT, AND A COLORFUL PERSONALITY

Place of origin US	
Date of origin 1960s	
Breed registries CFA, FIFe, GCCF, TICA	
Weight range 8–12 lb (3.5–5.5 kg)	
Grooming	

Colors and patterns
Various colors, some with silver tipping; tortie pattern; silver hairs always ticked.

This astoundingly beautiful breed is a longhaired relative of the Abyssinian (p.83). Neither the Somali nor its short-coated relative have any proven links with Africa to justify their names. The eye-catching coat of the Somali comes in a variety of rich colors and is exceptionally fine-haired. Most striking of all of the cat's features is its immense, bushy tail. Lively and insatiably curious, the Somali makes an amusing and engaging pet. Though highly affectionate and family friendly, this is not generally a lap cat; the Somali has too much energy to sit still for long.

Eyes encircled by lighter color

Dark markings on cheeks and brow

Rich-colored coat known as "ruddy," with distinctive ticking

Slightly arched back

Almond-shaped eyes have dark rim

Large, round-tipped ears set well back on skull

Fine-haired, ruddy coat with very soft texture

Rounded muzzle

Long, bushy tail resembles a fox's tail

Muscular yet graceful body

BRITISH LONGHAIR

THIS CHUNKY, HANDSOME CAT HAS A LONG, FLOWING COAT

Place of origin	UK
Date of origin	1800s
Breed registries	TICA
Weight range	9–18 lb (4–8 kg)
Grooming	

Colors and patterns
Same colors and patterns as recognized in the British Shorthair.

This cat, known as the Lowlander in the US and the Britanica in Europe, is the longer-haired cousin of the British Shorthair (pp.68-77). The two are identical in body shape, sharing the same sturdy build, massive head, and round face, and both come in the same range of colors. Not all pedigree cat registries regard the British Longhair as a separate breed. Regardless of its official status, this cat makes an excellent pet, since it has a calm, easygoing, people-loving temperament. The long coat needs moderate grooming to keep it tangle-free.

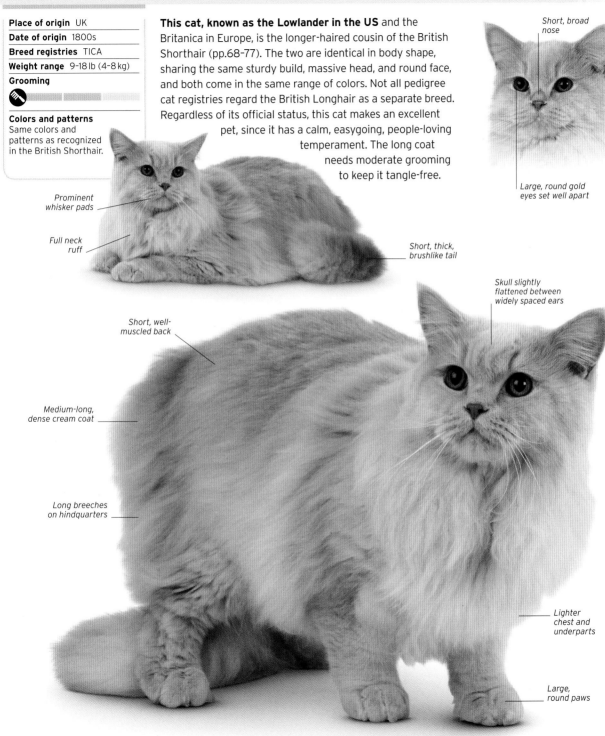

Short, broad nose

Large, round gold eyes set well apart

Prominent whisker pads

Full neck ruff

Short, thick, brushlike tail

Skull slightly flattened between widely spaced ears

Short, well-muscled back

Medium-long, dense cream coat

Long breeches on hindquarters

Lighter chest and underparts

Large, round paws

NEBELUNG

AN AFFECTIONATE BREED THAT LIKES A SECURE ROUTINE AND IS SHY WITH STRANGERS

Place of origin	US
Date of origin	1980s
Breed registries	GCCF, TICA
Weight range	6–11 lb (2.5–5 kg)
Grooming	

Colors and patterns
Blue, sometimes silver-tipped.

Developed in Denver in the late 20th century, the Nebelung is an outcross from the Russian Blue (pp.66–67), deliberately bred to recreate the longhaired blue cats that were popular in the Victorian era. The breed's name, taken from the German word *nebel*, meaning haze or mist, is appropriate to its softly glistening coat. Naturally reserved and preferring a quiet environment, this cat may not settle well in a family of boisterous children. However, with sensitive handling, the Nebelung makes a devoted pet, anxious to keep its owners in sight and loving a lap to sit on.

Feathering behind ears

Slightly oval yellowish-green eyes

Long, graceful body

Silver-tipped blue coat has soft sheen

Large ears continue wedge-shaped line of head

Prominent whisker pads

Heavily plumed tail

Ruff around neck

Shorter fur on lower legs

Hair tufts between toes

NORWEGIAN FOREST CAT

THIS CAT IS BIG, TOUGH, AND BURLY BUT ALSO GENTLE AND WELL-MANNERED

Place of origin	Norway
Date of origin	1950s
Breed registries	CFA, FIFe, GCCF, TICA
Weight range	7–20 lb (3–9 kg)

Grooming

Colors and patterns
Most solid colors, shades, and patterns.

Cats have been known in Scandinavia since Viking times, being kept as useful pest destroyers in homesteads and villages. The Norwegian Forest Cat cannot claim direct descent from these ancestors, since the breed was developed fully only in the 1970s, but its characteristics are recognizably those of the cats familiar for centuries on Norwegian farms.

This magnificent cat's long double coat, a natural insulation against bitter northern winters, may become much thicker in colder months as the undercoat reaches full density. Surprisingly, this does not mean extra winter grooming for owners, although shedding is likely to be heavy in spring.

Broad-based ears rounded at tip

Almond-shaped green eyes

Triangular head

Silver tabby coat

Nose straight in profile

Long, plumed tail

Well-muscled, powerful body

Short, strong neck

Thick silver patched-tabby coat

White markings on chest, face, and legs

Thick tufts between toes

TURKISH VAN

A PLAYFUL BREED WITH AN UNUSUAL LIKING FOR WATER GAMES

Place of origin Turkey/UK (modern breed)

Date of origin Pre-1700

Breed registries CFA, FIFe, GCCF, TICA,

Weight range 7-19 lb (3-8.5 kg)

Grooming

Colors and patterns
White with darker colors on head and tail.

The predecessors of this cat, named after the Lake Van area of eastern Turkey, may have existed for hundreds of years around the region now known as the Middle East. The modern Turkish Van was first developed in the UK in the 1950s, and breeding cats have since been exported to other countries, though they remain uncommon. A Turkish Van is not the ideal choice for an owner who wants a peaceful lap cat–zestful and fun-loving, this cat enjoys a game, especially if the family joins in. Many Turkish Vans also love dabbling about with water, and some are reputed to be confident swimmers.

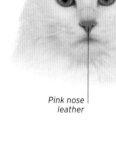

Pink nose leather

Ears set well apart

Soft, water-resistant white coat has no undercoat

Large amber eyes with pink rims

Auburn Van markings restricted to head and tail

Prominent cheekbones

Feathered tail

Broad, well-muscled body, especially in males

Deep chest

Long legs with fairly large, rounded paws

TURKISH VANKEDISI

THIS RARE BREED IS AN ALL-WHITE VARIANT OF THE TURKISH VAN CAT

Place of origin	Eastern Turkey
Date of origin	Pre-1700
Breed registries	GCCF
Weight range	7–19 lb (3–8.5 kg)

Grooming

Colors and patterns
Pure white only.

This cat has its origins in the same region of Turkey as the Turkish Van (opposite), and it is distinguished from that breed only by the lack of the typical Van markings on its snow-white coat. In all other respects, it shares the characteristics of its relation. The Turkish Vankedisi is rare anywhere in the world and is much prized in its native country. Like many all-white cats, the breed has a tendency to inherit deafness, but it is nonetheless strong and active. Its pleasant temperament makes this cat an affectionate companion, but it demands plenty of attention.

Long, straight nose

Silky, snow-white coat

Long hair inside ears

Fairly broad, wedge-shaped head

Odd-colored eyes

Pink rim around eyes

Long, muscular legs

Long, bushy tail

Round, tufted paws

TURKISH ANGORA
THIS BREED IS DELICATE TO LOOK AT BUT HAS A STRONG CHARACTER

Place of origin	Turkey
Date of origin	16th century
Breed registries	CFA, FIFe, TICA
Weight range	6–11 lb (2.5–5 kg)

Grooming

Colors and patterns
Many solid colors and shades; patterns include tabby, tortoiseshell, and bicolor.

Records indicate that this native Turkish breed probably reached France and the UK sometime around the 17th century. Widely used in the development of other longhaired cats such as Persians, especially during the early 20th century, the Turkish Angora as a breed became so diluted that it almost ceased to exist except in its own country. In Turkey, the cat had been given greater protection, and by the 1950s, purebred Angoras were being sent around Europe and to the US. Still rare, the Angora is one of the most exquisite of all longhaired cats, with its fine bone structure and exceptionally soft, glistening coat.

Small- to medium-sized head

Blue-cream coat

Fine-boned, slender yet muscular body

Slender, graceful neck

Small, rounded paws usually tufted between the toes

Large, tufted ears set high on head

Almond-shaped, slightly slanting green eyes

Fine, silky, shimmering black coat, with no undercoat

Long, tapering, brushlike tail

Long legs

SIBERIAN

A LARGE, HEAVY-COATED CAT THAT IS SLOW TO REACH FULL MATURITY

Place of origin	Russia
Date of origin	1980s
Breed registries	CFA, FIFe, GCCF, TICA
Weight range	10–20 lb (4.5–9 kg)

Grooming

Colors and patterns
All colors and patterns.

This forest cat is native to Russia, where it has probably been around for centuries in varying forms. Breeding Siberians to standard did not begin until the 1980s, and full breed recognition did not come until a decade later after a number of cats had been imported to the US. Although still rare, the Siberian cat is gaining popularity for its handsome looks and engaging personality. It may take five years or more for a Siberian to attain full growth. Despite its moderately hefty build in adulthood, this breed is highly athletic and loves to leap and play.

Round-tipped ears tilt slightly forward

Short, well-rounded muzzle

Unique triple coat

Thick ruff around neck

Eyes almost round, slightly angled toward base of ear, and may be different colored

Silver-spotted tabby coat

Tail shorter than body length

White markings on chest, face, and legs

Limbs heavily boned

Large, round, tufted white paws

NEVA MASQUERADE

A MAGNIFICENT COLORPOINTED CAT WITH AN ULTRA-THICK COAT

Place of origin	Russia
Date of origin	1970s
Breed registries	FIFe
Weight range	10–20 lb (4.5–9 kg)

Grooming

Colors and patterns
Various colorpoints, including seal, blue, red, cream, tabby, and tortoiseshell.

This breed is the colorpoint version of the Siberian (p.179), a forest cat that has a long history in Russia. The Neva Masquerade is named after the Neva River in St. Petersburg, where it was first developed. Combining strength with gentleness, this substantially built cat makes an excellent family pet and has a reputation for becoming particularly attached to children. The immensely thick coat of the Neva Masquerade, which has a double-layered undercoat, is not inclined to form mats or knots, so grooming is not a difficult task, although it does need to be done regularly.

Tufted ears set to side of head

Broad, round muzzle

Dense white ruff around neck

Substantially boned, strong, muscular body

Darker ears and mask

Large, slightly oval blue eyes

Blue tabby pointing on tail, legs, and head

Very thick, long, weatherproof, triple coat

Tabby markings evident on legs

Long, fluffy haunches

Large paws tufted between toes

MUNCHKIN

A DEVOTED CAT WITH VERY SHORT LEGS BUT A FULL ZEST FOR LIVING

Place of origin	US
Date of origin	1980s
Breed registries	TICA
Weight range	6–9 lb (2.5–4 kg)

Grooming

Colors and patterns
All colors, shades, and patterns.

The extraordinarily short legs of the Munchkin are the result of a chance mutation. This breed appears to have escaped the spinal problems sometimes associated with very short legs in dogs such as the Dachshund, and having a low-to-the-ground stature does not inhibit its general mobility. In fact, Munchkins can run extremely fast and are energetic and playful. These confident and inquisitive cats make sociable family pets. As well as the silky, semi-longhaired version, there is also a shorthaired Munchkin (p.101), and both come in an almost endless variety of colors and patterns. The Munchkin longhair needs regular grooming to prevent the coat from matting.

Flat forehead

Walnut-shaped golden eyes, set wide apart, have an alert expression

Muscular body

Whisker pads often prominent

Exceptionally short legs

Ears with slightly rounded tips

Well-defined cheekbones

Silky, weather-resistant coat

Tail is same length as body, with rounded tip

Back with slight slope from shoulders to rump

Shaggy haunches

MINUET
THIS SHORT, ROUND CAT COMES WITH A LUXURIOUS FUR COAT

Place of origin	US
Date of origin	1990s
Breed registries	TICA
Weight range	7–17lb (3–7.5kg)
Grooming	

Colors and patterns
All colors, shades, and patterns, including colorpoint.

A sturdy, low-to-the-ground cat, the Minuet longhair (formerly called Napoleon) is a hybrid specially bred to combine the very short legs of the Munchkin (p.181) with the luxuriant fur of the Persian (pp.136–155), including versions with a colorpointed coat. There is also a shorthaired variant of the Minuet. This breed is very active, despite its short stature, and has plenty of character. The Persian influence has ensured that the Minuet likes spending time as a lap cat too, and it loves to be made a fuss of, although it is not overly demanding.

Round head with full cheeks

Round, wide-open eyes

Smallish ears with rounded tips

Muzzle fairly short with round whisker pads

Ruff around neck

Semi-long white coat stands out from body

Short nose with well-defined stop

Long, plumed tail

Shaggy breeches

Short, firm legs

SCOTTISH FOLD

A CHARMING, SOCIABLE CAT WITH A DELIGHTFUL OWL-FACED APPEARANCE

Place of origin UK/US

Date of origin 1960s

Breed registries CFA, TICA

Weight range 6-13lb (2.5-6kg)

Grooming

Colors and patterns
Most solid colors and shades; most tabby, tortie, and colorpoint patterns.

The tightly folded-down ears of this rare breed and its shorthaired relation (pp.106-107) are due to a genetic mutation seen in no other cat. Descended from a folded-ear Scottish farm cat, the Fold is not recognized as a breed by the leading cat registry in the UK because of concerns about genetically linked health problems, although it has been more successful in the US. The diverse coat colors of the Scottish Fold come from the many different outcrosses, including domestic non-pedigree cats that were selected to develop the breed. The dense coat is of variable length and is enhanced by a thick ruff and a huge, plumed tail.

Rounded golden eyes

Prominent whisker pads

Long, plumed tail

Medium-sized, well-padded body

Small ears fold tightly forward to fit over skull like a cap

Thick ruff, especially with winter coat

Tufted toes

Rounded head with firm jaw

Long, full blue-cream and white coat

Short, broad, slightly curved nose

White markings on legs extend to chest and face

Long, plumed tail

Moderately strong yet slender body

Seal tortoiseshell point with white coat

Tufted ears curl backward

Walnut-shaped eyes

Rounded muzzle

Fine, silky coat with very little undercoat

Medium-length legs

AMERICAN CURL

A RARE BREED WITH HIGHLY DISTINCTIVE CURLED-BACK EARS

Place of origin	US
Date of origin	1980s
Breed registries	CFA, FIFe, TICA
Weight range	7–11 lb (3–5 kg)
Grooming	

Colors and patterns
All solid colors and shades; patterns include colorpoint, tabby, and tortoiseshell.

This breed has its origins in a stray cat with a long, black coat and oddly curled ears that was adopted off the street by a family in California in 1981. The cat, a female, went on to produce a litter of curly eared kittens, and the rare mutation aroused widespread interest among both breeders and geneticists. Programs for the planned development of the American Curl, in both longhaired and shorthaired (p.109) variants, began remarkably quickly, and the future of the new breed was secured.

In an American Curl, the ears curve backward to a greater or lesser extent, the arc of the curl ideally somewhere between 90 and 180 degrees. The cartilage is firm, not floppy, and the ears of these cats should never be manipulated. At birth, all Curl kittens have straight ears, but in about 50 percent of them, the characteristic curve begins to take shape within a few days, reaching its full arc by the time the cat is about 3 or 4 months old. Cats whose ears remain straight are of value in breeding programs, because their use helps keep the American Curl genetically healthy.

The longhaired Curl has a silky coat that lies close to the body. There is very little undercoat, which makes grooming easy and means minimal shedding. A further embellishment in the longhair is the lovely, long, plumed tail.

Alert, intelligent, and affectionate, the American Curl has an attractive personality and is an excellent family pet. This cat is gentle and soft-voiced but not at all shy about pestering its owner for attention.

HIGHLANDER

THIS RARE BREED WITH STRIKING LOOKS IS FAMILY-LOVING AND PLAYFUL

Place of origin North America
Date of origin 2000s
Breed registries TICA
Weight range 10-25 lb (4.5-11 kg)
Grooming

Colors and patterns
All colors in any tabby pattern, including colorpoints.

With its thick, almost shaggy coat, the Highlander longhair looks like a small lynx, although there are no wild cats in its breeding. This curly eared newcomer on the cat scene is large and powerfully built but moves with grace. Full of life and energy, the Highlander longhair is not content to stay in the background, and owners—and other pets—will be pestered constantly to play. Nonetheless, this is an affectionate, gentle cat that gets along well with children. The heavy coat needs regular grooming to prevent mats and tangling. There is a shorthaired version (p.109) of the Highlander that is easier to maintain.

Sloping forehead

Prominent whisker pads

Long, soft, chocolate-spotted tabby coat

Substantial, well-boned legs

Curled ears

Naturally short tail is curled

Long, strong, flexible hindlegs

Nose and muzzle look blunt in profile

Longer, lighter hair on belly

Medium to large paws thickly tufted between toes

NEW LOOK
Just created in the 21st century, the Highlander is not yet well known. With appealing shaggy looks, quirky ears, and a fun-loving nature, the breed has great potential for future popularity.

JAPANESE BOBTAIL

THIS CAT IS ALWAYS ON THE GO, TALKATIVE, AND INQUISITIVE

Place of origin	Japan
Date of origin	c.17th century
Breed registries	CFA, TICA
Weight range	6–9 lb (2.5–4 kg)

Grooming

Colors and patterns
All solid colors in bicolor, tabby, and tortie patterns.

Both longhaired and shorthaired (p.110) Japanese Bobtails appear to have been favored pets in Japan for several hundred years. In the 1960s, the first of these charismatic and unusual cats were imported to the US, where the modern breed was developed. Japanese Bobtails are loving and lovable, but with their outgoing and energetic natures, they are not for the owner who wants a lap cat. There are many variations on the short, plumed tail, which can curve or bend in any direction. The longhaired coat falls softly over the body and is relatively easy to groom.

Large, oval eyes set at a slant

Long nose with slight stop

Unique kinked bunny tail

Long coat parts along top line

Brown mackerel-tabby coloring

Elegantly sculpted head with high cheekbones

Ears set wide apart

Longer coat on hindquarters

Hindlegs longer than forelegs

Soft, silky white coat with minimal undercoat

Long, slender legs with oval paws

KURILIAN BOBTAIL

A RARE SHORT-TAILED BREED THAT THRIVES ON COMPANY AND AFFECTION

Place of origin Kuril Islands, North Pacific

Date of origin 20th century (modern breed)

Breed registries FIFe, TICA

Weight range 7–10 lb (3–4.5 kg)

Grooming

Colors and patterns Most solid colors, shades, and patterns, including tabby.

This solidly handsome cat takes its name from the Kuril Islands, an archipelago in the North Pacific, where it is thought to have its origins. As both Russia and Japan have laid claim to various of these islands, it is uncertain from which country the Kurilian Bobtail longhair really comes. The breed has been popular on the Russian mainland since the 1950s, as has the shorthaired version (p.111), but it is uncommon elsewhere and particularly rare in the US. The Kurilian Bobtail adores family life and can never get enough fussing and attention from its owner, although it has a strong streak of independence.

Bright, oval gold eyes

Prominent whisker pads

Body large but compact and well proportioned

Short tail is kinked

Medium-sized ears wide at base

Large, rounded head

Cobby body shape

Silky, semi-long red-silver mackerel tabby coat

Banding on legs

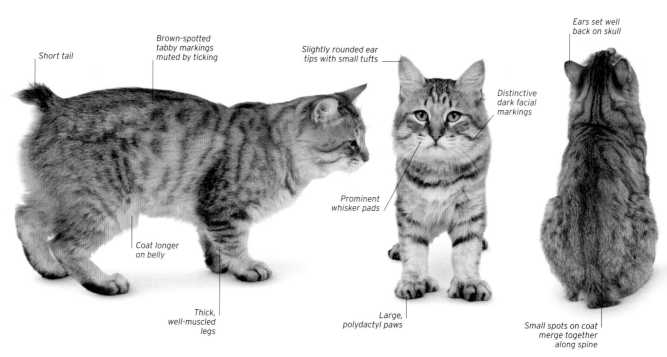

Short tail

Brown-spotted tabby markings muted by ticking

Slightly rounded ear tips with small tufts

Ears set well back on skull

Distinctive dark facial markings

Prominent whisker pads

Coat longer on belly

Thick, well-muscled legs

Large, polydactyl paws

Small spots on coat merge together along spine

PIXIEBOB

THIS LARGE BREED RESEMBLES THE WILD BOBCAT OF NORTH AMERICA

Place of origin	US
Date of origin	1980s
Breed registries	TICA
Weight range	9–18 lb (4–8 kg)

Grooming

Colors and patterns
Brown spotted tabby only.

This relatively new breed has a similar appearance to the bobcat, native to the mountains of the Pacific coast. The resemblance is deliberate—the Pixiebob's characteristics having been developed by breeders catering for a growing fashion in domestic cats that look like their wild cousins. Lynxlike features include a thick, double tabby-spotted coat that stands out from the body; tufted ears; a heavy brow; and facial hair that grows in sideburns. The tail varies in length and may be long and brushlike, although only short-tailed cats are eligible for showing. A shorthaired variation of the Pixiebob (p.116) creates much the same wildcat illusion.

The founding father of this breed was an exceptionally tall, bobtailed tabby that bred with an ordinary domestic female cat, siring bobtailed kittens with a special look—one of them, christened Pixie, passed her name to the breed.

Powerfully built, with a swaggering air, Pixiebobs are active and athletic. However, they are also relaxed and sociable cats that take happily to family life, enjoy playing with older children, and are usually tolerant of other pets. Pixiebobs like being with people, and many enjoy outdoor walks on a lead.

FAMILY CHARACTERISTICS

The kitten seen below has its mother's short hair but the bobtail and polydactyly (extra toes) of its longhaired father (main photos). This is the only breed in which polydactyly is allowed in show cats.

CYMRIC

AN EXCELLENT FAMILY COMPANION, THIS BREED IS CALM BUT EASILY PERSUADED TO PLAY

Place of origin	North America
Date of origin	1960s
Breed registries	FIFe, TICA
Weight range	8–12 lb (3.5–5.5 kg)

Grooming

Colors and patterns
All colors, shades, and patterns.

Developed in Canada, the Cymric is a longhaired variant of the tailless Manx (p.115). Sturdy and round-bodied, the breed, which is sometimes referred to as the Longhaired Manx, differs from its relative only in the length of its silky coat. Muscular hindquarters and long hindlegs give the Cymric a powerful jump–it can spring up onto high places with ease. Cymrics have an affectionate nature, frequently forming close attachments to their human family. They make intelligent and entertaining companions and appreciate plenty of attention from their owners.

Prominent whisker pads

Ruff around neck extends to shoulders

Thick breeches on hindlegs

Coat shorter on lower legs

Short back slopes gently down toward rump

White, glossy double coat lies smoothly on body

Large, round eyes slightly angled

Well-rounded rump lacks tail

Well-muscled hindquarters and legs

Sturdy forelegs shorter than hindlegs

AMERICAN BOBTAIL
A WILD CAT LOOKALIKE WITH A HOME-LOVING PERSONALITY

Place of origin US

Date of origin 1960s

Breed registries CFA, TICA

Weight range 7–15 lb (3–7 kg)

Grooming

Colors and patterns
All colors, shades, and patterns.

According to a widely accepted opinion, the origins of this true native American cat can be traced to the naturally short-tailed, feral cats found roaming free in various US states. The breed also has a short-coated cousin (p.113). The large, powerfully built Bobtail longhair has the alert air of a wild cat, but it is entirely benign and a good family pet. It is renowned for being tolerant of children and staying calm and friendly even with strangers. The Bobtail's long coat does not mat, so moderate grooming is all that is required.

Distinct brow above eyes

Alert "wild cat" expression

Chocolate spotted tabby coat

Short, slightly curved tail

Large, deep-set, almost almond-shaped eyes

Nonmatting, easy-to-groom, classic brown tabby coat

Well-built, muscular body

Hips as wide as chest

Prominent whisker pads

Legs substantially boned

SELKIRK REX

THIS BREED HAS WILD CURLS AND AN ENDEARINGLY HUGGABLE PERSONALITY

Place of origin	US
Date of origin	1980s
Breed registries	CFA, FiFe, GCCF, TICA
Weight range	8–11lb (3.5–5kg)

Grooming

Colors and patterns
All colors, shades, and patterns.

The breed originated with an odd curly coated female kitten, discovered among an otherwise normal litter in an animal rescue center in Montana. Adopted as something of a curiosity, this cat went on to produce curly offspring and lay the foundations for the Selkirk Rex. Through planned matings with both Persians and short-coated breeds, longhaired and shorthaired (pp.124–125) lines were developed. These sweet-tempered, placid cats are almost irresistibly cuddly, and fortunately they are very happy to accept attention. Regular grooming of the Selkirk Rex longhair is essential, but owners should avoid overvigorous brushing, because this can straighten out the curls.

Nose has well-defined stop

Round-cheeked, broad head

Short, square muzzle with full whisker pads

Longer white ruff around neck

Thick tail with rounded tip

Large, round blue eyes

Straight back rises slightly toward rear

Brittle curly whiskers

Medium-large, heavily boned body

Soft, loose, seal and white curls cover entire body

Large, round white paws

URAL REX

A LITTLE-KNOWN BREED, THIS CAT IS SAID TO BE QUIET AND GOOD WITH FAMILIES

Place of origin	Russia
Date of origin	1940s
Breed registries	Other
Weight range	8–15lb (3.5–7kg)

Grooming

Colors and patterns
Various colors and patterns, including tabby.

Although this cat was not generally recognized until fairly late in the 20th century, it is possibly one of the oldest of the rex breeds and is thought to have been in existence in the Ural region of Russia since the late 1940s. The Ural Rex longhair has a medium-long coat that falls in waves over its entire body. This rare cat comes in a shorter-haired version (p.122), which is also far from common. As test breeding has shown, the genetic mutation responsible for the Ural Rex's wavy coat appears to be very different from that found in other, better-known, rex cats, such as the Cornish Rex (p.127) and Devon Rex (pp.128–129).

Ears have rounded tips

Large, slanted, oval eyes

Pronounced cheekbones

Relatively short, muscular body

Slim legs

Tail tapers to rounded tip

Short, broad, wedge-shaped head

Oval white paws

Semi-long chocolate coat lies in loose, elastic waves

LAPERM

THIS CLEVER AND CAPTIVATING CAT ADORES HUMAN COMPANY

Place of origin	US
Date of origin	1980s
Breed registries	CFA, FiFe, GCCF, TICA
Weight range	8–11lb (3.5–5kg)

Grooming

Colors and patterns
All colors, shades, and patterns.

An ordinary farm cat in Oregon produced the curly coated kittens that led to the development of the LaPerm. The unique coat of this shaggy but graceful cat varies considerably from soft waves to bouncy, corkscrew curls. There is also a shorthaired version (p.123). Long-legged and agile, LaPerms are active cats, but will readily accommodate their owners by switching from playing games to purring on a lap. The LaPerm is not difficult to groom, because it has very little undercoat to shed or mat. Regular combing is the best way to keep the curls in good order.

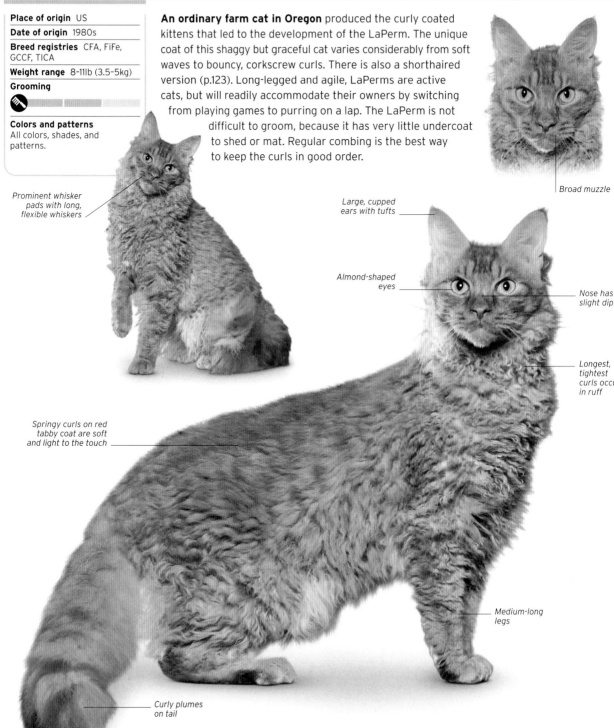

Broad muzzle

Prominent whisker pads with long, flexible whiskers

Large, cupped ears with tufts

Almond-shaped eyes

Nose has slight dip

Longest, tightest curls occur in ruff

Springy curls on red tabby coat are soft and light to the touch

Medium-long legs

Curly plumes on tail

HOUSE CAT–LONGHAIR

REGARDLESS OF THEIR ANCESTRY, THESE CATS HAVE UNDENIABLE GLAMOUR

Nonpedigree cats with long hair are less common than their shorthaired counterparts. In some of them, the clues to their origins are obvious. A dense, woolly undercoat; a stocky body; and a round, flattened face are likely to be inherited from a Persian. The ancestry of others remains a mystery in a confusion of variable coat lengths, mixed colors, and indeterminate patterns. Longhaired house cats rarely have the extravagantly thick coats seen in the show ring, but many of them are very beautiful.

BROWN TABBY
Long fur tends to blur tabby patterning. This cat has a semi-long coat marked with the pattern known as classic tabby, which on a shorter coat would appear as boldly defined, dark whorls.

Faint tabby markings

Greenish-gold eyes

Brownish tinge to ruff

CREAM AND WHITE
Cream—a diluted form of red—is an unusual color in the average house cat. This one has ghost tabby markings, which cat fanciers try to eliminate in pedigrees by breeding only the very palest creams.

BLACK
Jet black was among the first colors to be popular in longhairs. In random-bred cats, there are likely to be slight tinges of brown or tabby pattern in the coat.

Thick, medium-long hair on body

RED AND WHITE TABBY
Most owners of a red tabby are likely to refer to their pet as a ginger cat. This color is highly sought after and can often be just as deep and rich in nonpedigree cats as it is in purebreds.

Round face suggests Persian influence

SILVER AND WHITE
Rarely seen in the domestic house cat, silver is the effect of a white coat tipped with darker color at the end of each hair. Depending on their degree of tipping, pedigree silver cats are sometimes known as chinchillas.

CARE AND BEHAVIOR

PREPARING FOR ARRIVAL

Is your house ready for a cat or kitten? Before bringing a new pet home, take a good look around and ask yourself a few key questions: Is there anywhere you don't want your cat to go? Is there anything that could be hazardous to a cat? Which of your own habits might you or your family need to change when you have a cat? A little preparation will turn your home into a safe environment for the new arrival.

A kitten is life-changing

Become cat aware

Cats are inquisitive and athletic, and you should take this into account when evaluating your home. If you regularly leave doors and windows open, assess whether your cat could escape through them or enter areas you want to keep cat-free—and close them when necessary. Also, start looking behind you when going through a door, since a cat can easily slip through a gap at your feet. Close the doors of washing machines and dryers when not in use, and always check the whereabouts of your cat before switching them on.

Safety indoors

Cats love climbing, so remove breakable or valuable objects from low tables or shelves that they could leap onto. Be aware of possible pathways that would allow your cat to reach high shelves or work surfaces, and move furniture accordingly. Stools, floor lamps, wall hangings, and curtains are all scalable to a cat. Consider temporarily putting double-sided sticky tape, plastic sheeting, or aluminum foil around the edges of furniture you want to remain off limits until your cat learns to leave them alone; cats dislike these textures and will avoid stepping on them. Climbing and scratching are entirely natural behaviors for a cat, so make sure you provide outlets for these activities, such as a scratching pole and something safe for him to climb on.

TOP TIP

Household chemicals are an obvious hazard. Keep them securely shut away in places a cat cannot reach. Mop up spills right away. Also check whether any products are toxic to cats—for example, carpet cleaners and bug control sprays. Do the same in any garage or shed that a cat could access. Even seemingly innocuous substances may be dangerous to cats, especially since their first instinct is to lick themselves clean if they get something on their coat or paws.

WINDOW SCREENS
Using window screens will enable you to leave windows open for fresh air and in hot weather, safe in the knowledge that your cat cannot escape.

OUTDOOR THREATS

FOXES

SNAKES

OTHER CATS

FIREWORKS

SUNBURN
(WHITE CATS)

TOP TIPS

■ **Keep your cat indoors** during firework displays. Close doors and windows, mask the noise with music, and let your cat hide if he wants to. Don't reassure him—this may be taken as a sign that you, too, are afraid. A pheromone plug-in may help your cat stay calm.

■ **Cat sunblock** can be bought from pet shops. Cats with white coats or patches of white are susceptible to sunburn, since the skin under the fur is also pale. Use only cat-friendly sunblock.

and their claws, but they may harm kittens. Snakes are an issue in some places, mainly because cats prey on them and sometimes get bitten in the process. There are cat-friendly snake-repellent products on the market. Always examine your pet carefully after a fight with a neighborhood cat, in case he has injuries that need a vet's attention. In urban areas, the greatest threat will be from traffic, so do your best to prevent your cat from being able to reach the road.

Dangerous plants

Some plants are toxic to cats if eaten (see below). Remove these dangerous plants from the garden. Keep houseplants off the floor and low tables, and cover the soil with bark chips or pebbles to discourage digging. If your cat must nibble indoors, buy special cat grass plants from nurseries and keep them away from other plants to avoid confusion.

NATURALLY CURIOUS
Cats will inspect and explore whatever and wherever they can. Make sure cupboards cannot be opened, and always put away sharp knives, scissors, pins, and tacks.

Beware of leaving small objects lying around: cats can swallow or choke on things such as toys, bottle caps, pen tops, and erasers. Tuck away wiring on electrical appliances and pull up dangling cords so your cat cannot drag a lamp or iron onto himself. Fit unused electrical sockets with childproof covers.

Safety outdoors

After assessing your home, carry out a "safety audit" of your garden and yard. Remove sharp, potentially harmful objects and prevent access to sheds and greenhouses. Even if you try to secure your yard from animal intruders, you will always have some "visitors." Foxes are usually wary of mature cats

DANGEROUS PLANTS

INDOORS		OUTDOORS
■ Dieffenbachia	■ Cactus	■ Azalea
■ Poinsettia	■ Potted bulbs–	■ Hydrangea
■ Mistletoe	crocus, daffodils	■ Nightshade
■ Lily	■ Philodendron	■ Oleander
		■ Nicotiana
		■ Tomato leaves
		■ Potato leaves
		■ Rhododendron
		■ Yew
		■ Monkshood

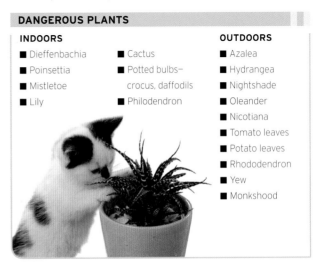

Equipment for your cat

If you are a new cat owner, you'll need to buy a certain amount of equipment for your pet's comfort and well-being. These items include a bed, a litter box, feeding and drinking bowls, and a scratching post. It's tempting to go for the latest "must have" items, but think carefully about whether your cat really needs such things. Start with good-quality basic items that are within your budget, because the initial outlay on your cat will quickly mount up. You can think about treating him to more products later on.

Bed and bedding

Felines will take a catnap anywhere that captures their fancy, but like most animals, they really appreciate somewhere that is exclusively their territory. Choose a round or oval, washable, soft-sided bed that is not too big. A blanket or old cushion can be added if your cat is not yet fully grown.

HANGING AROUND
Suspended from a radiator, this cat bed provides your pet with a warm, cozy place to sleep.

Basket style

Tent style

CAT BEDS
Beds come in a wide range of styles. If you know what kind of bed your cat used before joining your family, choose that type; otherwise, try to match the bed style with what you know of his character.

Litter boxes

Open, covered, manual, automatic, self-cleaning–the choice of litter boxes is ultimately up to you. However, if you are acquiring an older cat, stick to the type of box with which he is familiar: a cat used to an open box, for example, is likely to be reluctant to change to a covered one. Choosing the right litter material may involve some trial and error before you find a brand that your cat likes using and that meets your own requirements for cleaning. You can also add deodorizers to the litter. These come as sprays, powders, or granules; avoid scented products, since these may deter your cat from using the box. The best deodorizers use enzymes to break down smells. A plastic scoop will be useful for removing clumps of urine and feces from the litter. Always wash the scoop after using it.

Litter box

Scoop

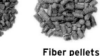

Clay   **Fiber pellets**

WHICH LITTER TO CHOOSE?

■ **Ask the breeder** which litter the kitten is used to and stick with the same type.

■ **Clay** is the most popular type of litter, because it absorbs moisture quickly and clumps are easy to remove.

■ **Fiber, wood, and paper** pellets are very absorbent products and are biodegradable.

■ **Nonabsorbent** litter needs to be used in conjunction with a special box that drains the urine into a collecting unit. This is useful for collection of urine samples should a vet ask for one. Feces need to be removed and disposed of, but the litter material itself can be washed and reused.

■ **Soil and sand** are popular choices for most cats. However, they are bulky to store and are not biodegradable.

Food and water bowls

Bowls should be sturdy and stable enough not to tip over if stepped on. They should be shallow, wider than the cat's whiskers, and made of steel or glazed ceramic. Wash bowls at least once a day. Remove "wet" food after the cat has finished eating. If you feed your cat canned food, buy an extra can opener that you can reserve solely for opening cat food. Use plastic lids for any partially used cans stored in the refrigerator. There are also automatic feeding stations available that operate on a timer. They flip open a lid at your cat's mealtime—a useful asset if you are going out and don't want to break the cat's routine.

Scratching posts

Providing a place for your cat to scratch is essential if you don't want your furniture or carpets ruined. Cats need to scratch every day to help wear away the outer sheaths of their claws. Scratching is also a way of marking territory. Scratching posts are usually a flat, rough-carpeted base and an upright post covered in coiled rope, often topped by a carpeted platform (p.235). Make sure the post is tall enough for your cat to get a really good stretch—preferably at least 1ft (30 cm) high. Locate the post close to where your cat usually sleeps, since cats do most of their stretching and scratching immediately after waking up.

Collars and ID

It is important to get your cat tagged with a microchip. These tiny devices are no bigger than a grain of rice and are inserted by a vet under the loose skin at the back of the neck. Each chip has a unique number that can be detected when it is scanned by a reader. When the number is fed into a database, your contact details will come up. It's worth doing this even if you have an indoor cat—cats are experts at escaping and may take advantage of an open window or a loose door on a cat carrier. All outdoor cats should have

Glazed ceramic **Steel**

a collar with an ID tag giving your name and address, along with a telephone number or email address. The collar must be loose enough for you slip two fingers underneath. Many collars have an elasticized section or quick-release snap that allows the cat to escape if the collar becomes snagged.

Cat carriers

A cat carrier is the safest way to transport your cat. Whether it is made of plastic or wire or is a traditional basket, it must be large enough for your cat to turn around in. A blanket or cushion can be put inside to keep him warm and comfy. To get your cat used to traveling in a carrier, keep the carrier open and in a place that he can access and use as a refuge. If he regards the carrier as a place of safety, he will be happier to travel in it—even when it results in a trip to the vet.

Cat carrier

CARRIER CRITERIA
A good cat carrier will be easy to enter and exit. It will shield your cat from the outside but still let in plenty of fresh air and light and allow him to see out.

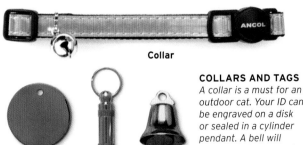

Collar

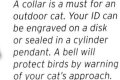

Disk tag **Cylinder tag** **Bell**

COLLARS AND TAGS
A collar is a must for an outdoor cat. Your ID can be engraved on a disk or sealed in a cylinder pendant. A bell will protect birds by warning of your cat's approach.

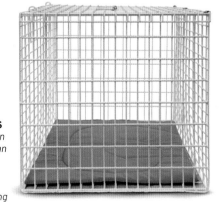

Cat cage

CAGE OPTION
An open cage may be more suitable if your cat doesn't like the confines of a carrier. While a carrier will sit well on a car seat, a cage may have to be put securely in the back of a large car.

FIRST DAYS

A new family member

Moving to a new home can be as strange an experience for a new cat or kitten as it is for a human. Although a cat will quickly adapt to his new surroundings, you should aim to make his first few days in an unfamiliar household as calm and stress-free as possible. To aid this, some advance planning and a course of action implemented by the entire family can help him feel at ease.

Thinking ahead

Plan to bring your cat home on a day when your house will be very calm and quiet, so that you can devote all your attention to him. If you have children, explain to them that their new pet will be a little scared at first and that they should give him time to get used to them. Don't let them get overexcited about this new addition to the family. If you've never had a family pet before, try to make your children understand that the cat is not a toy and will need to be kept calm for the first few days.

Transporting your cat

Your cat or kitten needs a secure box or cat carrier to be transported safely. If possible, put a piece of his bedding into the carrier so that he recognizes the familiar smell. Cover the carrier if necessary so that he can only see out of one end; this will help reduce his anxiety. Strap the carrier into the car seat with a seatbelt or place it on the floor to prevent your cat from being thrown if you have to stop suddenly.

> **TOP TIP**
>
> **Some cats are bolder** than others. If your cat leaves the carrier quickly and appears confident, try introducing a toy and playing with him for a while. This will help break the ice and make your cat feel more relaxed in his new home.

FIRST STEPS
A cat will feel more in control if you let him emerge when he wants. If you force him out, you will merely succeed in causing anxiety.

Welcome home

When you arrive back at your house, bring your cat into the room where he will be spending his first few days. It's best to restrict him to one or two rooms until he is settled. Check that any doors and windows are closed. If you already have other pets, make sure they are out of the way in another room. Put the carrier on the floor and open the door. Allow your cat to venture out in his own time; be patient, and do not try to remove him yourself. Curiosity will eventually get the better of him, and he will leave the carrier and start to explore.

Showing your cat the ropes

Part of your cat's acclimatization involves introducing him to the essential elements of his new life: his basket, litter box, feeding area, and scratching post. Make sure that these are in easily accessible places but are away from busy areas of the house. It is best to start with the litter box—with any luck, your cat will use it right away. If the box is in a separate room, make sure that he can always get to it. Feeding bowls should be put in a place where it is easy to clean up any spills.

Meeting the residents

It will be hard to keep small children away from something as exciting and cute as a new cat or kitten. However, too much yelling, shrieking, and rushing around may frighten your cat, so make sure they understand this. Show them how to hold your cat correctly (p.216) and let them stroke or cuddle him, but if he starts looking unhappy, then be swift to intervene and take control—a nasty scratch could put a child off of their new pet for a long while. Perhaps think about providing children with an activity or treat that will keep them out of the way for an hour or two after they have been introduced to their new pet, so as not to overwhelm him. Also, make them aware that what they leave on the floor could be dangerous to their new kitten— such as small toys—and that they will need to look where they're going from now on to avoid stepping on him.

WHAT'S MY NAME?

Think carefully about what you are going to call your cat. Cats respond best to short, one- or two-syllable names. Make sure it sounds different from the names of any other pets or even members of the family, so that he will learn to recognize his own name and come when called.

INTRODUCTIONS

When showing a new cat to a child, always keep ahold of him. Children need to learn how to handle a pet, so let them follow your example.

Start as you mean to continue

Establish the ground rules from the outset, especially about feeding and sleeping. If you give your cat morsels from your plate, for example, he will always expect tidbits and may even refuse his own food. Make sure everyone in the house knows and sticks to the rules. A cat will not understand if you allow him to do something one day but not the next.

BEDTIME RULES
If you allow your new cat to sleep on your bed at night, that is where he will always expect to sleep in the future.

READY FOR A NEW HOME
Kittens are used to the warmth and companionship of littermates and may be timid on their own. Given love and patience, your new cat will soon become a confident member of the family.

Establishing a routine

Cats are creatures of habit. Setting a routine in the early days will help your cat or kitten to settle into his new home and make him feel secure. Eventually, your cat will develop his own patterns of behavior around your family's daily schedule.

Base your routine around regular activities such as feeding, grooming, and playtime. You will need to be consistent with this for several months, so make sure it fits in with your own commitments and habits. Cats do not like constant change—it can stress them and may result in behavioral problems such as digging, chewing, biting, and general hostility. A regular routine will also help you notice any changes in your cat's behavior and health. Predictability means safety to your cat.

Decide on regular mealtimes for your cat, and always put the bowls in the same place. By doing this, you can keep an eye on his appetite, and it will also prove useful for training to know when he's hungry.

If your cat needs regular grooming, aim to do this at the same time each day. Grooming may not be your cat's favorite activity, but it will be tolerated if your pet knows it's only going to take a limited amount of time. Grooming just before mealtime or playtime will give your cat an incentive to be close by and to cooperate with the process.

Having a regular playtime is also a good idea. It gives your cat something to look forward to and reduces the likelihood of "mad hours," when your cat goes crazy and rushes around the house or won't leave you alone. Make sure that playtime is a worthwhile experience with plenty of variety and a decent amount of time devoted solely to the cat.

TOP TIP

Plan when you will give your cat his first feeding. You won't want your cat howling for its 6 a.m. weekday breakfast on a Saturday or Sunday if you like sleeping in on the weekend. If you train a cat to eat at a certain time, stick to your side of the bargain—feed him at the same time every day.

REGULAR MEALTIMES
Giving your cat meals at set times of the day is just one of many routines that will help him adjust to his new home.

PREPARING THE LITTER BOX
Make sure the litter box is set up and ready for use by the time you bring your cat home—you never know how soon it may be needed.

LITTER SHARING
The general rule is one litter box per cat, but if you start them young, they may accept a shared box.

TOXOPLASMOSIS

Cat feces may contain the parasite *Toxoplasma gondii.* Humans can be infected by *T. gondii* from contact with cat feces, contaminated soil, and cat litter. The infection, called toxoplasmosis, may produce a flulike reaction, but in most cases, there are no symptoms at all. However, it is dangerous for pregnant women to come into contact with cat feces, because the infection can be passed to the unborn baby. In extreme cases, this can result in problems as serious as blindness and brain damage.

Litter box etiquette

Most cats and kittens will already know how to use a litter box by the time you bring them home, but an unfamiliar box or litter product may cause a few problems in the early stages. A cat used to one type of litter may not like changing to another. Use the same litter as the breeder initially, so the cat first has a chance to get used to the litter. Then you can make the change to the new product gradually by mixing the two types, adding a greater proportion of the new product each time you change the litter.

If your cat is avoiding the litter box, try setting up another box containing a different product to see which he prefers. Generally, the finer the product feels under his paws, the more attractive it will be to a cat, which is why most instinctively go for sand or soil. Keep the litter box in the same place all the time and within easy access. If the location is too busy, your cat may refuse to use his box—cats like their privacy, too. Clean the box out regularly. Scoop out clumps every day and change the litter once a week. Rinse the box well after washing to remove any lingering chemical smell, and resist the temptation to mask litter odors with scented sanitizers or deodorants.

Coping with change

There will always be times when routines have to change. Some changes can be positive experiences for your cat, so long as they don't make him feel threatened or stressed. There will inevitably be occasions when you have to go out for the day and leave your cat on his own, which will disrupt his usual playtime or grooming sessions. It won't matter if you have these sessions before you go out or when you

come back instead, or even abandon them completely, but try to make a fuss over your cat at some point and leave him with toys so that he can entertain himself.

Going on vacation

Vacations are always tricky times for cat owners, and you will need to organize things so that your cat's routine remains as constant as possible. Cats can adjust to their owner being away or being taken to a new place, but rarely to the two happening at the same time. The best option is to ask a friend or relative to come in and feed your cat at home. If this is not possible and you have to resort to professional pet sitters, then make sure you ask for references.

Boarding kennels can be stressful places for cats, so it's vital to choose a good one. Ask cat owners whose judgment you trust if they can recommend any. Go and visit the kennel before using it to see conditions for yourself. They should have a license from the proper authority—don't be afraid to ask to see it. Remember to book well in advance, especially if the kennel is popular.

VACATION HOME
A good boarding kennel will have separate sleeping and exercise areas for each cat, without allowing contact between the animals.

FOOD AND FEEDING

A well-fed and well-nourished cat is a happy cat. Although the occasional mouse caught outside may supplement your cat's diet, he will rely on you almost exclusively for his food. And that reliance places great responsibility on you. Providing your cat with a healthy, balanced diet will help him grow and develop as he should and give him the best chance of living a long life free of illness.

**Eating healthily
for a long life**

Essential nutrition

Cats are carnivores—they eat meat because they cannot convert the fats and proteins found in vegetable matter into the amino acids and fatty acids necessary for their bodies to function properly and stay healthy. Meat protein contains everything they need plus an important amino acid that they cannot make—taurine. Insufficient taurine in a cat's diet can lead to blindness and heart disease. Taurine is added to all processed cat foods. Cooking reduces its effectiveness, so if you cook your cat's food yourself, you will also need to provide him with a regular taurine supplement.

Vitamins and micronutrients

The vitamins needed for essential cat nutrition include D, K, E, B, and A. (Cats cannot manufacture vitamin A.) They also need vitamin C, but intake of this vitamin should be monitored, since cats can develop bladder stones if they have too much. Cats also require certain micronutrients—for example, phosphorus, selenium, and sodium. Although these are only needed in tiny quantities, a lack of them can lead to serious health problems. A source of calcium is vital, too, because calcium only occurs in small quantities in meat. Most commercial cat food contains all of these essential vitamins and micronutrients.

Wet or dry?

Most prepared cat food is described as "wet" or "dry." Wet food comes in airtight cans or pouches, so it doesn't need preservatives to keep it fresh. It is tasty but soft in texture, so it provides little resistance to keep teeth and gums healthy. If wet food is not eaten immediately, it will soon become unappealing to your cat.

Dry food has been pressure-cooked and then dried. It is sprayed with fat to make it palatable, but this requires preservatives to be added. Dry foods usually include antioxidants such as vitamin C and E, which are natural and beneficial to your cat. Although you shouldn't give your cat dry food all the

FIBER FROM PREY
Cats require a source of fiber to maintain healthy digestive function. In the wild, they obtain the fiber they need from the fur, skin, and feathers of their prey.

Dry food

Wet food

Home-cooked

WET, DRY, AND HOME-COOKED FOOD
Dry food won't spoil, but wet food is more like a cat's natural diet. Homemade meals are freshest, but avoid single-protein diets.

time, it does have some advantages. It can, for example, be left out during the day without spoiling. You may want to give dry food in the morning and reserve the wet food for when you return from work in the evening.

Home-cooked food

For home-cooked meals, use meat and fish that's fit for human consumption. Make sure it is well cooked to kill bacteria or parasites that could be dangerous. Homemade meals are a good way of introducing well-cooked bones as a calcium source, but don't offer them if your cat has not learned to eat bones or if he eats his food too quickly. The scraping action of bones keeps teeth in good shape; without them, your cat's teeth will need regular cleaning (p.231).

Drinking requirements

All cats should be provided with a source of water, since water helps dilute the urine and is absorbed by fiber in the gut. Caution should be taken with giving cats milk or cream, since many adult cats lack the enzyme necessary to digest

the lactose sugar in dairy products and may get diarrhea. Special "cat milk" can now be bought; alternatively, use milk for lactose-intolerant humans available at supermarkets.

Foods to avoid

As well as milk and cream, other foods to avoid include raw fish, which contains enzymes that can be harmful to cats. Onions and garlic can cause anemia, while green tomatoes and green (raw) potatoes—and especially their leaves—contain a poisonous alkaloid that produces violent gastrointestinal symptoms, so keep these items out of reach. Chocolate is highly toxic to cats, and grapes and raisins may harm the kidneys.

DRINKING WATER
Cats fed a dry-food diet will require more water than those that eat wet food.

DANGEROUS FOODS

Onions and garlic

Green tomatoes and potatoes

Chocolate

Grapes and raisins

Cream

Raw fish

When and how much to feed

Generally, your cat should be fed twice a day at regular times. This will allow him to build up an appetite and you to regulate how much he eats. Once you have established a regular feeding regime, it will be easy to tell if your cat is not eating and feeling unwell. The feeding guides printed on packets of prepared food are only estimates, and they may

CAT GRASS
Cats eat grass because its juices contain folic acid, which prevents anemia. Cat grass bought from a pet store or nursery can be grown indoors in a small pot.

EATING THE RIGHT AMOUNT
If you have more than one kitten, make sure that they are all eating the right quantity for their age and weight. If you suspect one isn't eating enough, try feeding him separately so that you can monitor his intake.

need to be increased or decreased depending on how your cat looks and feels when handled. As a guideline, you should be able to feel your cat's ribs easily but not see them. Make sure you never feed an adult cat kitten food or dog food– kitten food contains too much protein and will be bad for an adult cat's kidneys; conversely, dog food does not contain enough protein for a cat. Make sure your cat's food and water bowls are always washed thoroughly after use.

The right balance

Cats enjoy variety, and it is important that they are fed a mix of different foods to ensure they get adequate nutrition. Make any changes to your cat's diet gradually so that he can build up enough bacteria in his system to digest the new food. Once you've found a balanced diet that your cat likes, stick to it. Constantly changing his food may encourage him to become a fussy eater, and cats can hold out for days until you give them what they want.

Special diets

Your cat's dietary needs will change throughout his life. Kittens need lots of protein, fat, and calories to support their rapid growth. Use specially formulated kitten food to avoid deficiencies that could cause problems later in life. For the first week after bringing your kitten home, give him the same food that he has eaten since weaning. To introduce a new food, replace 10 percent of the original food with the new food, increasing the proportion by 10 percent daily until your kitten is eating only the new food by the tenth day—this will prevent diarrhea. If he does get an upset stomach, revert to a higher proportion of the old food and take longer to make the switchover.

A pregnant cat needs extra protein and vitamins and will want to eat more in the final stages of pregnancy. This may mean giving her smaller meals more frequently if she cannot eat as much as usual at a time. She will also have increased nutritional requirements when nursing. Older cats use less energy, so they need fewer calories in their diet. They may need special food to aid a more delicate digestive system.

For cats with medical conditions and overweight cats, use a diet recommended by your vet. An approved weight-loss diet ensures that an obese cat loses weight but stays nourished and still eats a satisfying volume of food. Food allergies in cats are rare, but when they occur, the only way to find the cause is through a food-elimination trial supervised by your vet.

The role of treats

Whether given as rewards in training or to aid bonding with your cat, try to ration treats to avoid weight gain in your cat. Ensure that 10 percent maximum of your cat's calorie intake comes from treats. Some treats may give nutritional benefits that your cat won't get from his normal food; others contain filler ingredients with little nutritional value and a lot of fat. Learn to distinguish good ingredients from bad.

IT'S TREAT TIME
Rewards for learning new tricks will reinforce training, while treats given when you leave for work and return home can be something your pet looks forward to.

WHICH TREAT?
Treats come in many different meat and fish flavors. Whatever you choose, make sure you don't overfeed your cat.

FEEDING YOUR CAT

ADULT WEIGHT		4.5 LB	9 LB	13.5 LB	22 LB	26.5 LB
Inactive lifestyle		100–140 cal (4 oz wet/1 oz dry)	200–280 cal (8 oz wet/2 oz dry)	300–420 cal (12 oz wet/3 oz dry)	400–560 cal (16 oz wet/4 oz dry)	500–700 cal (20 oz wet/5 oz dry)
Active lifestyle		140–180 cal (6 oz wet/1.5 oz dry)	280–360 cal (12 oz wet/3 oz dry)	420–540 cal (16 oz wet/4 oz dry)	560–720 cal (24 oz wet/6 oz dry)	700–900 cal (28 oz wet/7 oz dry)
Pregnant female		200–280 cal (8 oz wet/2 oz dry)	400–560 cal (16 oz wet/4 oz dry)	600–840 cal (24 oz wet/6 oz dry)	800–1,120 cal (32 oz wet/8 oz dry)	1,000–1,400 cal (44 oz wet/11 oz dry)

HANDLING YOUR CAT

Cats are notoriously choosy about who they will allow to touch them, let alone pick them up and pet them. Some cats simply don't like being picked up and will struggle to get free. There are right and wrong ways to handle a cat—learn how to do it properly and your cat will enjoy the opportunity to get closer to you. If he's comfortable with being held, it will be easier for you to groom him and check for injury or illness.

A correctly held kitten

STRESS-BUSTER
There's something about cats that makes us want to stroke them. Research has shown that petting cats is good for reducing stress in humans—and cats like it, too.

Start early

The best time to get a cat used to being handled is when it is a kitten. Early and routine contact from about 2 or 3 weeks old helps kittens not only develop faster, but also grow into more contented cats that are happy to be handled by humans. If you have children, teach them to be gentle and to treat the kitten with respect. Mistreated and mishandled kittens will grow into nervous cats who keep their distance from people and who are difficult to train. Cats have long memories, and they will avoid children who handle them too roughly or pull their tails.

How to pick up a cat

A very young kitten can be picked up by the scruff of his neck, like his mother does, but he will need more support as he gets older and heavier. When his mother stops picking him up like this, so should you. From then on, the correct way to pick up your cat will be to approach from the side and place one hand flat against his ribcage, just behind his front legs. Use the other hand to support him under his hindquarters.

CARRYING YOUR CAT
Don't cradle your cat on its back when you pick him up—this position is unnatural to a cat and will make him feel vulnerable. Instead, try to hold him as upright as possible. Put one hand under the "armpits" of his front legs, place the other under his rear, and hold him securely.

TOP TIP

Never try to pick up a cat that doesn't know you. First, let him sniff and investigate you. Try stroking him while talking in a calm tone—if he gets used to you being friendly, he may be happy to be picked up in the future. If he seems nervous, back off. Sudden movements could make him lash out, then run off. Treat feral or fully wild cats with even more caution.

Different strokes

Try not to stroke your cat unless he is willing to be touched. Put out a hand or finger for him to sniff. If he touches you with his nose or rubs his cheek or body against you, he's in the mood for contact. If he shows no interest, leave it until another time.

Once your cat is amenable to being petted, begin by stroking him along his back in a slow, continuous motion. Always go from head to tail, never the other way. Stop when you reach his tail. If your cat is enjoying it, he may arch his back to increase the pressure of your hand.

Learn how your cat likes to be petted. The top of the head, especially between and behind the ears, is often a favorite place. Cats can't reach this spot, and it reminds them of when their mother used to lick them there. Some cats also like being stroked under the chin. Rubbing the cheeks with a circular motion is popular with many cats, because it helps them spread their scent onto your fingers.

HEAD SCRATCHING
Scratch with the pads of your fingers from back to front. Be slow and gentle—cats can be fussy about how they are petted.

Your cat may like being raked with the fingers, but don't stop and scratch him in one place. Most cats dislike being patted, especially along the flank. When your cat jumps into your lap and lies down, pet him once to see if he wants attention or just a warm place to snooze. If he fidgets or his tail twitches, stop stroking. A cat that is enjoying being petted may change his position so that the part he wants stroking is uppermost and closest to your hand.

Rough and tumble

Some cats like rough play and will grab and "play bite" at a hand that tries to rub their belly. If your cat sinks his claws in, keep still until he disengages. Pushing farther in toward him may surprise him enough to let go. In general, when you stop, so will he. If he kicks with his back legs at your hand, don't assume that he wants his paws touched. Try stroking one foot lightly with a finger in the direction of his fur; if he pulls his foot away, flattens his ears, or walks off, let him be.

Knowing when to stop

Watch your cat's body language and stop stroking if he seems to be getting angry (pp.224–225). Be careful if he is on his back exposing his belly because this is not necessarily an invitation to pet; it may be an aggressive defense posture that leaves him free to kick, bite, or claw. If you misjudge his mood and get a bite or a scratch that breaks the skin, wash the wound and treat it with antiseptic. See your doctor if the area around the bite swells and starts oozing.

CAT MAKING CONTACT
Your cat may often make the first move himself by bumping or brushing up against you. If it's not convenient for you to pet him, at least stroke your cat once or twice so he knows he's not being ignored.

SOCIALIZING YOUR CAT

Dogs and cats need not be archenemies

By nature, cats are solitary creatures. That said, some cats are able to live quite happily in groups. Bringing a new cat into your home may change his whole outlook on the people and other animals around him. But if introductions are made carefully and sensitively, your cat will grow into a confident, friendly animal that can cope with all social situations.

Start early

Socialization should start in kittenhood. Give your kitten plenty of opportunities to meet new people, cats, and dogs, and make it a fun and rewarding experience. Introduce him to friends, neighbors, and the vet at an early age; keep initial encounters brief and reward your kitten with treats for good behavior. A cat that is not exposed to new situations as a kitten may grow up to be timid and fearful and is liable to react badly to being touched or approached by strangers.

Kittens start to learn social skills from their mother between 8 and 12 weeks of age. Be wary of bringing home a kitten younger than this; otherwise, his socialization will be your responsibility. It is important that your kitten gets used to being handled, with plenty of play designed to hone his predatory skills, but let him sleep when he wants to. Kittens left to spend a long time on their own without stimulation or attention may develop antisocial behaviors and grow up to be aloof or aggressive toward people and other animals.

Socializing an adult cat

Adult cats take longer than kittens to adapt to new people and surroundings. Changes in routine are upsetting for an older cat, and unless you are familiar with your cat's previous home, there may be issues related to how he has

OLDER AND CALMER
If you have very small children, it may be better to get an adult cat. Toddlers may not realize how gently they need to handle a kitten, while an older cat may be more tolerant of children.

SOCIALIZING MOTHER
Adopting a kitten less than 12 weeks old is not often recommended—it still needs a lot of socialization time with its mother, who will teach it essential life skills.

been treated in the past. Try to get as much information as possible from the previous owner or rescue center about the cat's personality, habits, motivations, and favorite food and toys. Familiar objects can also help him settle in, so try to bring some of his old bedding or toys to make him feel more secure. Provide him with a refuge, such as a carrier or box, to which he can retreat and feel safe when things get too overwhelming.

An older cat may initially be wary of contact with his new owners and may resist being touched. Let him explore his surroundings in his own time. Talk to him in a low, soothing tone so that he gets used to your presence and the sound of your voice. Gradually accustom him to being handled by rewarding him with treats. One of the main problems with poorly socialized cats is that they play too rough, biting and scratching to get what they want. If that is the case, simply stop playing with him, say "no" in a firm voice, and give him a toy instead. If your cat learns that biting or scratching achieves the outcome he wants, it will be difficult to get him to break the habit. Give plenty of praise when your cat is playing nicely with you, but also praise him when he takes his aggression out on a toy. That way, he will learn that he can play hard with toys but not with you.

New people need to be introduced with care. Never force your cat to meet strangers. Instead, let him approach the person when he is ready; once he realizes that nothing bad is going to happen, he will be more confident and trusting. You can speed up the process by laying a trail of treats up to the stranger. This works best when your cat is hungry. (You can also restrict treats to occasions when there is a visitor in the house.) When your cat is comfortable with the person, a friendly stroke or two on the head or back can be attempted. If you have to leave your cat to be looked after by friends or neighbors, get him used to the new people in advance. Ask them to come to your home frequently to feed him treats and pet or play with him. He will soon look forward to their visits.

Introducing children

If you have small children, your cat may feel threatened and frightened by their exuberant, noisy behavior and sudden movements—especially if they chase him. His preferred defense will be to run away, but when cornered, he may respond by hissing, scratching, or biting, all of which may scare or hurt a small child. It pays to prepare your children for the cat's arrival by reading through a book about cat care with them. First meetings should be supervised, especially if toddlers are involved. Let your cat or kitten take the initiative and approach the child. If he decides to flee, let him go. Play sessions should involve the child sitting still on the floor with a lure toy or ribbon that encourages the cat to come closer.

To make your children feel involved, give each responsibility for some aspect of the cat's care, such as filling the water bowl, shaking out the bedding, putting his food away, or collecting his toys. To avoid overfeeding, make sure only one child has the job of feeding your cat. Never let a young child clean out your cat's litter box. Cat feces can carry intestinal parasites, such as worms, and an infection called toxoplasmosis that can be harmful to a young child (p.211).

A new baby

If your cat has always been the center of attention, he may become jealous of the competition for affection when a new baby arrives. Some careful preparation can help prevent this. Before the birth, allow your cat to examine the baby's room and gear, but make it clear that he is not allowed in on his own and that the crib, bassinet, and stroller are distinctly off limits. If you have friends or family with a baby, ask them to visit so that your cat becomes familiar with the sounds and smells. To accommodate the new domestic situation, you may need to change your cat's routine or how much time you will be spending with him. Introduce such changes gradually in the months leading up to the birth. Likewise, if your cat has any behavioral problems that you need to put right, now is the time to do it, since they may get worse when the baby arrives.

GETTING USED TO CHILDREN
A new cat will be an irresistible attraction to any children in your family. Teach them the correct way to approach and handle a cat, and make sure you supervise their initial encounters.

A NEW COMPANION
The arrival of a new baby need not cause problems for your cat if you get him used to the idea well in advance of the birth.

When you bring the baby home for the first time, allow your cat to sit next to the baby and give him treats for good behavior so that he associates the baby with a positive experience. Never leave the baby and cat alone together. Close the door to the room where your baby is sleeping or buy a screen to cover the door frame. You can also get nets to put over cribs and strollers, which will deter your cat from trying to snuggle up to your baby or from spraying if he is stressed. Try to keep your cat's routine as normal as possible and make sure he gets his share of attention from someone in the family.

Cats and dogs

Whether you are introducing a new cat to a dog or a new dog to a cat, the same methods of socializing them can be used, with slight modification. When you first bring your new cat home, put him in a room that the dog does not need to access until the cat has settled in. Alternatively, put up a barrier or put the dog in a crate. While the cat is getting used to his new surroundings, let the dog smell the cat's scent. You can do this by rubbing the dog with a towel that you have previously rubbed on the cat or letting the dog sniff your hands after handling the cat. Do the same with the cat. Once the dog is familiar with the cat's scent, put the dog on a lead and bring him to the door of the cat's room. Do not allow any bad behavior such as barking, scratching, or lunging. If the dog behaves properly, try letting him off the lead.

For the next stage of socialization, allow the dog through the door while on the lead, or put him in a crate in the cat's room. Let the pair sniff each other, but remove the dog if he attempts to jump on or chase the cat. Supervise encounters until the cat is comfortable around the dog. Initial contacts should be short and repeated several times a day. Praise and reward the dog for good behavior, so that he comes to regard the cat's presence in the house as a good thing.

Finally, you can try leaving the two alone in the room by walking out, then walking back in right away. Gradually extend the period of leaving them alone, but stay within listening distance. If you hear hissing, growling, or barking, return immediately. Make sure the cat has a safe place to hide that is out of the dog's reach. Continue this process until the dog no longer reacts to the cat and the cat is happy to eat or sleep when the dog is in the same room. Sadly, some dogs may never be safe to leave with a cat. If that is the case, you will have to keep them separate or supervise their encounters at all times.

Other cats in the home

Because your cat sees your home as his territory, bringing another adult cat into the house may be seen as a threat. A new kitten, however, is more likely to be tolerated by the resident. Keep a lookout for bullying and jealousy on the part of the adult cat. If it looks like the older cat is picking on the kitten, keep the two apart until the newcomer is more able to look after itself. Remember, this is the older cat's territory, and his natural instinct is to protect it from interlopers, however small. Make sure that the older cat gets his share of love and attention, and reward him with treats for good behavior. The two will gradually get used to each other and develop a companionable truce.

ACCEPTING ADULT
Adding a new kitten into the household does not usually threaten an adult cat's dominance. The older cat will most likely tolerate the kitten, understanding its playfulness to be part of its natural behavior.

LEARNING TO BE FRIENDS
Cats and dogs are not natural allies, but they can learn to get along. The dog must understand that the cat is not a toy. Make sure the dog does not get overexcited so the cat will feel safe when he is around.

INDOORS OR OUTDOORS?

One of the most important decisions you need to make before you acquire a cat is whether it is going to be a house cat or left free to roam the great outdoors. For many people, the decision rests on how "great" the outdoors would be for their cat. Owners need to take stock of their own lifestyle and their home's surroundings when deciding what is best for the long-term safety and happiness of their cat.

The freedom of the pet door

Call of the wild

Domestic cats were once wild animals, adapted to living in open spaces. Many of their wild instincts remain, but the world that cats inhabit has changed dramatically. Many cat owners live in urban environments, surrounded by busy roads, buildings, people, and other animals, and an outdoor cat will have to contend with all these hazards. In making your indoors-or-outdoors decision, the safety of your cat is paramount. Not all cats develop a good road sense, and some fall victim to passing cars. If you let your cat out at night, buy it a collar with reflective patches that can be seen in the dark by drivers. Cats are naturally more active at dawn or dusk—times that often correspond with rush hours. Try to keep your cat indoors at these times. Given the run of the neighborhood, your cat will probably explore beyond your yard, leading to encounters with other neighborhood cats and possibly wild animals, too.

WINDOW ON THE WORLD
If your cat is to be truly independent, install a pet door so that he can come and go as he pleases. Otherwise, you will be perpetually opening doors to see whether he wants to go out.

Creating cat heaven

The best way to keep an outdoor cat close to home is to make your yard a cat-friendly sanctuary. Plant it with bushes to provide shade and shelter and a few scented plants that cats love—such as catnip, mint, valerian, heather, and lemongrass—in sunny places for your cat to bask among. A clump of cat grass is ideal for your pet to snack on if you habitually spray your grass and plants with chemicals.

A PLACE IN THE SUN
Provide your cat with plenty of spots in the yard to bask and doze. A garden basket makes an ideal bed for a laid-back cat.

Territorial disputes

Once your yard is cat-friendly, it will undoubtedly attract other cats. Feline disputes are certain to break out, because cats are territorial animals. Make sure your cat is neutered—especially if she is female—to prevent unwanted pregnancies. Neutered cats need smaller territories, but that won't stop your cat from straying or an unneutered feral tomcat from invading your cat's territory and picking a fight. Make sure that your cat is immunized against all diseases, because fights will inevitably lead to bites and scratches.

Dealing with the neighbors

Appreciate that not all of your neighbors are cat lovers. Some people are allergic to cats and go to great lengths to avoid them. Even the best-trained cats have bad habits—they dig up flowerbeds to defecate, chew on plants, spray, rip open garbage bags, chase birds, and wander into other houses uninvited. If your cat has been neutered, tell your neighbor that neutered cats bury their droppings and that their urine is less smelly. You can always provide them with a water gun to squirt at the cat if they really want to deter it.

Indoor cats

Your cat will live a longer and healthier life if it stays indoors—but it will be your responsibility to keep it happy. If you are at work all day, your cat will need a regular playtime or, better still, a companion. Bored cats grow frustrated and stressed and can become overweight and unhealthy if they aren't exercised. Stress may manifest itself in scratching and biting or urinating outside the litter box. Despite their natural instincts, cats kept indoors from birth will rarely want to venture out, because they see your home as their territory. Once they get a taste for going out, however, they may want to do it more and more and look for any chance

KEEPING A CLOSE WATCH
Cats like to assume elevated positions from which they can watch over their territory. Shed roofs, fences, and pedestals—ideally in different parts of the yard—are perfect for this.

to escape. If so, you will have to be vigilant about closing windows and doors. Be extra careful in a high-rise apartment—many cats have died after falling from an open window or jumping off a balcony while chasing birds or insects.

Indoor cats need space to exercise, so they should have access to several rooms, especially if you have more than one cat—like us, cats need their own "personal space." To give your cat a breath of fresh air, you could screen off a porch, patio, or balcony that he can access through a pet door. Even if you live in an apartment building, allow your cat out into the hallway for a game that will allow him to run around. Ensure that any doors leading to the outside are closed first.

GOOD COMPANY
If they are not siblings, companion cats are best introduced early in their lives. They will provide company and a playmate for each other if you are out at work all day.

TOP TIPS

■ **With indoor cats,** you should always check where your cat is before leaving him alone in the house. Make especially sure you do not accidentally shut him away in a confined area such as a closet or cupboard.

■ **If you have** an outdoor cat, attach a bell to his collar to warn the wildlife in your garden of his presence. Bird baths and scattered food are a magnet for cats, so avoid leaving food out and keep bird feeders well out of reach of predatory cats.

CAT COMMUNICATION

You can always tell when a dog is happy or sad—its emotions are written all over its face. You will find your cat more inscrutable when it comes to facial expressions, so it may be difficult to know what your cat is trying to tell you. Cats do, however, have a whole range of other behaviors and signals that you can learn to interpret, which will make for much easier interaction between you and your cat.

Learn to understand your cat

How to speak cat

Wild cats are solitary, predatory animals that patrol a territory they regard as exclusively theirs. Consequently, most cat communications are designed to ward off intruders. Learning what your cat's body language, and the noises he makes, mean will help you understand what he is trying to tell you.

Chief among cat noises are hissing, growling, meowing, and purring. Hisses and growls—sometimes accompanied by a flash of teeth or show of claws—are warnings to strangers trespassing on the cat's territory or to humans who get too close. Meows—rarely used between adult cats—are mainly a way for kittens to signal to their mother. Domestically, your cat will use meowing to announce his presence. Short and high-pitched chirps and squeaks usually signal excitement or a plea for something, but drawn-out and low-pitched sounds express displeasure or a demand. Rapid, intense, and loud, repeated sounds often signify anxiety. Long, drawn-out cries and shrieks indicate that the cat is in pain or fighting. Mating cats produce long wails known as caterwauls. Purring is usually a sound of contentment, but cats also purr as a way of comforting themselves when they are in pain or anxious.

Body language

Your cat will give you signals using his ears, tail, whiskers, and eyes. Ears and whiskers usually work together. Normally the ears are erect and facing forward and the whiskers are to the front or sides, showing that your cat is alert and interested. When his ears are rotated back and flat and his whiskers are forward, he is feeling aggressive. Ears out to the sides and whiskers flat against the cheeks mean that your cat is scared.

Cats don't like eye contact, which is why your cat will often approach anyone in the room who ignores him; to him, this is friendly behavior. Once your cat is used to those around him, he will find eye contact less threatening. Dilated pupils can mean he is interested and excited or fearful and aggressive, so always try to read the other signals he is giving out, too.

INTIMIDATING EYE CONTACT
Cats use eye contact as a form of intimidation to avoid a fight. Staring is perceived as a threat, and two cats will try to outstare each other until one looks away or slinks off.

TOP TIPS

Speak cat, not human. If you hiss or make a spitting noise when you say "no" to unacceptable behavior, your cat will understand that it is doing something wrong. This will prove much more effective than yelling at him.

TAIL SIGNALS

The most obvious signs of your cat's mood are the visual signals he sends out. Although he will give you signals with all parts of his body, one of the best barometers of his emotional state is his tail. When you look at your cat, the way he is carrying and moving his tail will be a clear expression of the way he is currently feeling. Try to learn these different tail configurations and their meanings. Remember that his mood can change in an instant.

Flicking from side to side	Your cat is telling you that he is mildly irritated
Thumping on the floor	A sign of frustration or a warning signal
Curved like an "n" or low to the ground and flicking	With this tail-shape and action, your cat is advertising the fact that he is feeling aggressive
Strong lashing movements	Stand back—your cat is not happy and he may become aggressive if he's approached
Hair fluffed out and standing on end	A sign of increased anxiety and that your cat is feeling threatened
Arched over the back	A warning sign that he is poised ready to strike
Tucked between the legs	This tail position is a way of expressing submission
Horizontal or slightly low to the floor	Everything is all right—he is feeling calm and relaxed in a situation
Erect, sometimes with a curl at the tip	He is feeling friendly and interested in making contact with you
Pointing straight up and vibrating	Your cat is literally quivering with joy and excitement

Posture

Your cat's posture tells you one of two things: "go away" or "come closer." Lying, sitting in a relaxed manner, or coming toward you indicates that he is approachable. A cat on his back exposing his belly is not being submissive like a dog: this is usually a fight posture that allows him to wield all his claws and teeth. However, if he is also rolling from side to side, you can assume that he is in a playful mood. Avoid touching his belly too much, or you may get scratched or bitten. Wiggling the rump is another sign that he is up for some fun. When your cat is crouching—either looking sideways or with his tail wrapped around his body—he is looking for a chance to escape, pounce, or go on the offensive.

WARNING STANCE
When your cat stands with rump raised or back arched, he is feeling threatened and warning that he is about to attack. The hair on his body may also be raised.

CAT SPRAYING
Spraying is a perfectly natural behavior, and you should not punish your cat for doing it.

Smell and touch

Cats have a superb sense of smell, so they use urine and scent to mark territory and leave messages for other cats. A cat that is not neutered will spray to warn

of his presence, threaten any rivals, and announce that he is ready to mate. If a neutered cat still sprays, he is probably feeling anxious. Investigate what is triggering this behavior.

Cats also spread scent from glands on their cheeks, paws, and tail by rubbing them on surfaces or other cats. These scents mark territory and form social bonds. Cats that live together will rub each other along the flanks or the head, creating a group scent that alerts them to the presence of strangers. Your cat will also rub the members of your family to mark you all as part of his "gang." Cats sniff nose-to-nose when they meet; unfamiliar cats end the encounter there, but friendly cats progress to rubbing heads or licking each other's face or ears. Scratching is another way of leaving scent, as well as being a visual signal of a cat's presence.

THE IMPORTANCE OF PLAY

Playful kitten

No matter how pampered their existence, cats need some excitement in their lives. A cat deprived of opportunities to hunt and stalk becomes bored and stressed. This is a real problem with indoor cats, often locked up alone in a house all day. Yet, with forethought and commitment on your part, your cat can have an interesting and fun home life.

Going on instinct

Kept indoors alone all day, a bored cat will constantly pester you for attention when you get home. Outdoor cats have a riskier but happier and more active lifestyle. With plenty of fresh air, space to run and jump around, and exposure to new experiences, they can give free rein to their natural instincts for exploring, chasing, and hunting. Even when indoors, a cat will need to let off steam regularly. Often, this takes the form of a "mad moment," when the cat rushes around the room, leaping onto furniture and climbing the curtains before bolting off. This is perfectly natural behavior, but uncontrolled sessions like this run the risk of damaging your home and causing injury to your cat.

BORN FREE
A cat that cannot follow its instincts may become troublesome.

CONSTRUCTIVE PLAY | CHANNEL THE ENERGY

CHASING AND PLAYING
To prevent manic bursts of activity, channel your kitten's predatory instincts into constructive play. Dangling or dragging along a piece of ribbon will appeal to your kitten's natural urge to hunt and stalk.

CATCHING AND BITING
Play also helps your kitten learn essential skills for survival in the wild, such as catching and biting prey. Most cats, especially if neutered, will still retain their sense of playfulness as they get older.

TOP TIPS

■ **Supervise your cat's** use of anything that could be chewed or shredded and swallowed. Bits of string and fabric can cause intestinal blockages, while objects with sharp edges could damage your cat's mouth.

■ **Make sure** that curtain and window-blind cords are not allowed to dangle within reach of your cat, or he will view them as a great play opportunity. As agile as your cat may be, he could become entangled and suffocate.

Furry mouse

Fabric mouse with bell

Feather

Play balls

TOY PARADE
There is a wide range of playthings available for cats, from balls and pretend mice to catnip-scented toys. Many pet shops sell hollow balls in which a treat or small amount of food can be hidden.

Catnip braid

Toys

Cats like toys that appeal to their chasing, stalking, and pouncing instincts. Suitable toys include small, lightweight balls and beanbags; felt or rope mice; pom-poms; and feathers. Items dangled from poles are ideal for grabbing or batting with the paws and running after. Make sure that toys are in good condition, with no pieces that could fall off and be swallowed. Most cats find wind-up or battery-operated toys that move around the floor particularly exciting.

Cheaper options

You don't need to buy your cat expensive accessories or toys. Cats can make their own amusement from simple, everyday items such as crumpled newspaper, spools of thread, pencils, pine cones, corks, and feathers. Cats love hiding, so provide yours with somewhere to play hide-and-seek, such as an old cardboard box or paper bag. Never let a cat play with a plastic bag—a cat can suffocate inside or strangle itself if it gets trapped in the handles.

PLAY STATION
This multi-activity center provides plenty of variety for your cat, with a cozy hiding place, scratching posts, somewhere to sit, and hanging balls to play with.

EXPLORING AND HIDING
Paper bags appeal to a cat's sense of curiosity, giving him something to investigate and hide in. Monitor your cat and make sure he can get out whenever he wants to.

New tricks

One way to make playtime with your cat more interesting is to teach him a new trick (p.233). Unlike a dog, which will learn tricks to please its "pack leader," a cat needs a different motivator—food. The best time to teach your cat is just before a meal, when he is hungry. Select a quiet spot with no distractions, but don't spend more than a few minutes on each training session. You may need to repeat the training a few times each day for several weeks, depending on your cat's age and the difficulty of the trick. Reward your cat's progress in getting the trick right with small treats, and make sure you give him plenty of praise. Your cat will only be willing to participate if he is having a good time; don't try to force him to do something he doesn't want to, and don't get mad if he decides he isn't interested.

GROOMING AND HYGIENE

Cats instinctively groom themselves, spending much of their time keeping their fur clean, tangle-free, and conditioned. However, many cats, especially longhaired breeds, show cats, and older cats, will need some assistance from their owners. Helping out with basic hygiene, such as teeth cleaning and bathing, is also essential to keep your cat in peak condition.

A cat spends many hours grooming himself

Natural grooming

Grooming keeps your cat's coat in prime condition. This is important because a sleek, conditioned coat is waterproof, keeps your cat warm, and protects his skin from infection. Grooming can also help keep your cat cool in hot weather.

Your cat will always groom himself in the same order. He begins by licking his lips and paws, then using his wet paws to clean the sides of his head. The saliva removes the scent of recent meals, making him "odorless" to natural enemies that hunt by scent. Next, your cat will use his rough tongue to groom his front legs, shoulders, and sides. The tongue is covered in tiny hooks that can get rid of mats and tangles in the coat. The tongue also spreads the natural oils secreted by glands in the skin that condition and waterproof the coat. Your cat will nibble away any stubborn tangles using his small incisors. His flexible spine then allows him to attend to his anal region, back legs, and tail, working from its base to the tip. He then uses his back paws like a wide-toothed comb to scratch his head. Cats raised together may sometimes groom each other, strengthening the bond between them.

Grooming your cat

Helping your cat maintain his coat is essential for several reasons. Grooming sessions will enable you to maintain a close bond with your cat and also give you a chance to check his body for health problems. Some cats—especially those selectively bred for their long, soft hair, such as Persians—have difficulty keeping their coat clean and tangle-free on their own. When you groom your cat, you will help reduce the amount of hair he swallows while grooming himself. This hair is usually coughed up as fur balls. Some fur balls, however, pass through the stomach and get lodged in the intestine, causing serious problems. Cats become less efficient at grooming themselves as they get older, so elderly cats benefit greatly from a helping hand.

If you accustom your cat to grooming sessions from an early age, he will come to view you as a parent figure and enjoy the experience. Always begin a grooming session by stroking your cat and talking in a soothing voice to help him relax. Remember to be patient and on the lookout for signs that he is uncomfortable, such as a flicking tail or whiskers turning forward. In such cases, stop and try again later or the next day. Make sure you also check his ears, eyes, nose, and teeth, and clean them if necessary. You may also need to clip his claws, empty his scent-secreting anal sacs (or ask your vet to do this), and give him a bath. Always end a grooming session with praise and a treat.

GROOMING TOOLS
Basic utensils for cat grooming include combs (flea, fine, and wide-toothed), brushes (slicker, pin-tipped, or soft-bristled), a rubber grooming glove, clippers, a cat toothbrush, and a tick remover. Some breeds may require specific tools for their coat type.

Tick remover

Nail clippers   **Slicker brush**   **Fine comb**   **Soft-bristled brush**

GROOMING | SHORTHAIRED CAT

Shorthaired coats are easy to maintain, and most cats with such a coat cope well on their own, keeping their fur in tip-top condition. However, a once-a-week groom (twice weekly if you have a show cat) will help you maintain a close bond with your cat and allow you to check for any potential health issues, such as lumps or skin problems. Shorthaired cats generally benefit from a comb through with a flea or fine-toothed comb,

then a suitable brush or deshedding tool to clear out loosened hair and dead skin, and finally a "polish" with a soft cloth, such as a chamois leather or piece of silk to produce an eye-catching sheen. Take care when touching sensitive areas, such as the ears, armpits, belly, and tail. If your cat has rexed, or curled, hair, use a very soft brush or a rubber grooming glove—anything harder may cause discomfort.

LOOSENING OLD HAIR AND DEAD SKIN
Draw a fine-toothed, metal comb from head to tail, along the lie of the fur. This will loosen dead hair and skin cells. Be careful when grooming around the ears, the underside (armpits, belly, and groin), and the tail.

DEBRIS REMOVAL
Work over your cat's body with a slicker, soft-bristled brush, or deshedding tool again with the lie of the fur, to get rid of all the debris loosened by the combing. Finish by polishing with a soft cloth.

GROOMING | LONGHAIRED CAT

Longhaired cats need much more grooming than shorthairs, ideally 15–30 minutes per day. Long fur, especially if it is soft and downy, picks up dirt and tangles easily, particularly in the armpit, groin, and anal regions, and behind the ears. These tangles prevent the coat from protecting the cat properly, making the skin vulnerable to damage and infection.

The main aim of grooming longhaired cats is to eliminate the tangles. Cat talcum powder can help tease them out, but with severely knotted tangles the only solution is to cut them out with scissors. Make sure the scissor tips point outward, so that you do not cut the skin. If you are unsure about this, take your cat to a professional groomer or ask your vet to do it.

INITIAL COMBING
Comb the fur against the lie from the roots outward. Unscented talc will help tease out tangles and also remove excess oils. Work through again with a finer comb. Be careful combing the tail and underside.

BRUSHING OUT LOOSENED DEBRIS
Brush out loose debris and any remaining talc with a soft-bristled or pin-tipped brush. Work against the lie. Fluff out the coat with the brush or a wide-toothed comb. With a Persian, comb neck fur up into a ruff.

How to bathe your cat

Outdoor cats occasionally give themselves a dust bath, in which they roll in dry soil to clean their coat of grease and parasites, such as fleas. You can buy dry shampoo for cats, which works in a similar way. A shorthaired cat may need a wet bath if it becomes covered in oil or a pungent substance. A longhaired cat requires more frequent bathing. Few cats enjoy being bathed, and it's easier for both of you if you accustom your cat to the experience from an early age.

When bathing your cat, you will need to be patient. Use soothing words throughout the session and give treats to your cat afterward as a reward. Before you begin, close all doors and windows and make sure the room is warm and free of drafts. Prior to bathing your cat, brush his coat thoroughly. You can wash your cat in a bathtub or a sink using a shower attachment, but make sure the water flow is very weak. Line the bottom of the bath or sink with a rubber mat for your cat to grip, so he feels secure and will not slip.

GROOMING | BATHING A CAT

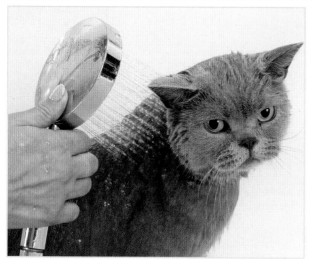

1 Lower your cat into a bathtub or place him in a sink, talking to him soothingly. Spray him with warm water that is as near to body temperature (101.5°F/38.6°C) as possible. Soak his fur thoroughly.

2 Always apply a special cat shampoo. Never use dog shampoo, since it might contain a flea-killing chemical that is toxic to cats. Avoid getting shampoo in your cat's eyes, ears, nose, or mouth.

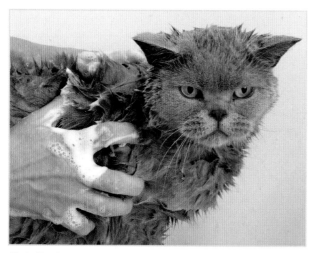

3 Lather in the shampoo thoroughly, then rinse it off completely. Repeat the shampoo wash or rub in a conditioner and rinse off again. Remember to keep giving your cat plenty of praise.

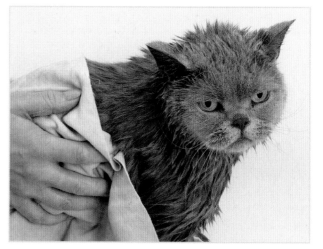

4 Towel dry your cat, or use an electric dryer on a low setting if the noise doesn't upset him. Brush his coat and allow him to finish drying off in a warm room. Give your cat a well-earned treat.

Cleaning ears, eyes, and nose

The inside of your cat's ears should be clean and free of odor. Remove excess earwax with cotton balls or tissues. If you see dark, gritty specks in the ears, which indicate ear mites, or an ear discharge, take your cat to the vet. Damp cotton balls can also be used to clean around the eyes and nose. Mucus may collect in the corners of the eyes of long-muzzled cats, such as Siamese. Flat-faced cats, such as Persians, often suffer from tear overflow, which leaves mahogany stains on the fur around the eyes. Consult your vet if you find any discharge from the eyes or nose or prolonged redness of the eyes.

TEETH CLEANING

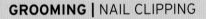

■ **Hold the head** firmly, pry open the jaws, and clean each tooth for a few seconds.

■ **Use a child's** toothbrush or a specially made cat's toothbrush, some of which fit onto a finger.

■ **Special cat toothpastes** are available. Your cat will especially enjoy the meat-flavored ones.

■ **If your cat** won't allow you to brush his teeth, ask your vet for oral antiseptics, which you apply directly to the cat's gums.

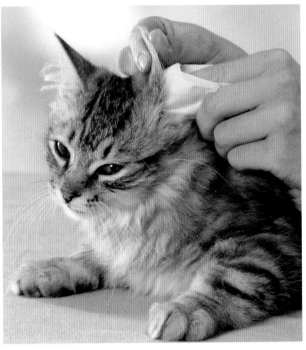

REMOVING EARWAX
Use a cotton ball or a tissue dampened with either water or an ear-cleaning solution from your vet. Never use cotton swabs, because you might push wax farther into the ear canal.

GROOMING | NAIL CLIPPING

How to clip your cat's nails

Cats naturally keep their nails worn down by exercise, scratching, climbing, and biting. Indoor and especially older cats often don't get much claw-wearing exercise and are at risk of growing long claws that curl into the pads of the paws, causing discomfort. To prevent this, regularly check your cat's claws and cut them with clippers about every two weeks. Keep a firm hold on your cat and make sure you remove just the very end of the claw. Any further down and you might cut into the pink region, or "quick," and cause pain and bleeding. If you find it too difficult, ask your vet to cut your cat's nails instead.

START THEM YOUNG
Accustom your cat to having his nails clipped from an early age. If your cat is not in the mood and struggles, don't force things. Let him go, and try again the next day.

EXTENDING THE CLAW
When clipping your cat's claws, very gently press down on the bone just behind each claw with your fingers to make the claw extend fully.

TRAINING YOUR CAT

Training your cat may sound like a strange, even impossible thing to do and contrary to the nature of such a free-spirited animal. But basic training, such as teaching your cat to sit, has benefits, and some cats make willing pupils. Training your cat will make it easier for you to control and manage his behavior. You may even be able to teach him a few tricks or train him to walk on a harness and lead.

Cat with harness

Anything for food

Cats are happy to learn if there's an edible reward. Unlike dogs, cats don't respond to discipline. Simply calling to your cat will not teach him to sit or come to you, but a tasty tidbit—such as a piece of dried salmon or a chicken treat—and lots of gentle praise will help greatly. Cats learn best when hungry; just before meals is ideal. During training, break treats into small portions. Too many too soon and your cat will stop feeling hungry and lose interest. Cats learn best from about 4 months old. Young kittens lack concentration; old cats are generally not interested. Active shorthaired cats, such as Siamese, are generally easier to train than other breeds.

COMING TO YOU
Teaching your cat to come to you on command is useful if you leave him outside during the day but want to bring him indoors at night or when you go out.

Basic training

Your cat cannot be trained unless he has a name—preferably a short name of one or two syllables that he will find easy to recognize and respond to. If you've adopted an adult cat, it's best not to change his name, even if you dislike it. Training sessions should last for one or two minutes, never much longer, and preferably in a quiet room, free of distractions.

To get a cat to come to you, call him by his name while tempting him with a treat. As he approaches, take a step back and say, "Come." When he has walked up to you, give the treat and praise him. Repeat this, increasing the distance each time until he will run to you from another room on hearing your command. If you then phase out the treats, he should still respond to your call.

Meow on cue

Once your cat has learned to come when called, you can try training him to meow on cue. Hold a treat in your hand and call to him, but withhold the treat until he meows—even if he tries to swipe the morsel from your hand. As soon as he does meow, say his name and at the same time hand over the treat. Practice both with and without giving a treat to reinforce the behavior, until your cat always meows at the sound of his name. You can then begin to phase out the treats.

ATTRACTING ATTENTION
When your cat can meow in response to his name, it will help you find him. It could even be a lifesaving skill if he becomes trapped somewhere.

LEARNING TO SIT
When your cat has learned to come when you call his name, you can then start to teach him to sit. If he can sit without fidgeting, it will be much easier to groom him or have him examined by a vet.

The sit command

To teach a cat to sit, place him on a table so that he is standing on all fours. Gain his attention with a treat and hold it a couple of inches above his head. If the treat is too far away, he will be inclined to rise up on his hindlegs and bat it from your hand. Slowly move the treat over your cat's head and between his ears, and as he watches it he will sit back. Say his name, then say, "Sit," as he begins to sit. Once he is sitting, say, "Good sit," and give the treat. After about 10 sessions, simply holding your hand over his head should be enough to make him sit.

Walking an indoor cat outside

You can give your indoor cat a taste of the outside world by walking him on a lead. Cats need a harness rather than just a collar, which they can easily slip their head out of. First, allow your cat to get used to wearing the harness. Put it on him for 20 minutes each day for a few days. Give treats and praise and make sure it fits correctly. Next, clip on the lead and let him stroll around indoors with it dangling, again for short periods, and then with you holding the lead. Finally, venture outside, ideally somewhere quiet. Your cat will initially spend most of his time sniffing and looking around and leading you. Never pull the lead in the direction you want to go; instead, persuade him with gentle commands and treats. Within a few weeks, he will be relaxed when walking with you outdoors.

Fun tricks

Once your cat has learned to come to you and to sit on command, you can go on to teach him some tricks, such as sitting up on his hindlegs, waving his paw, exchanging a high-five, retrieving thrown cat toys, or even jumping through a hoop. To get your cat to sit up or beg for example, hold a treat above his head and, when he rises, give the treat to him and say, "Good up." To get your sitting cat to high-five you, hold a teaser toy, such as feathers on the end of a stick, in front of him. As he raises his paw to the toy, say, "Good high-five," or "Alright!" and give him a reward. After several lessons, use your hand rather than the toy. Then gradually phase out the treats until you are just using clear hand signals and verbal cues.

The same principles apply for teaching tricks as they do for basic training: hold one- to two-minute sessions before meals, when your cat is hungry and willing to earn his food. Always remember to be patient and to give plenty of gentle praise. Don't try to persevere if your cat is not in the right mood.

THE WAVE
Cats can also master fun tricks, such as waving a paw, if you make the experience an enjoyable and rewarding one for them.

BEHAVIOR PROBLEMS

Pet cats sometimes have (what we humans consider) behavior problems, such as sudden aggression, scratching furniture, spraying urine, and refusing to use the litter box. Such actions make perfect sense—to a cat. Your job is to try to find out whether the behavior is caused by illness or stress, or just a case of a cat following his instincts. You will then, with patience, be able to solve or minimize the problem.

A stressed cat may be very destructive

Aggression

If your cat bites or scratches when you're playing with him, stop play immediately. He is probably becoming overexcited or does not want you touching a sensitive area, such as his belly. Don't use your hands as "toys" when playing with him, since it will encourage him to bite or scratch them. Rough play may trigger aggression, so make sure your children play gently and know when to leave him alone. Any pet dogs must be trained not to tease your cat to avoid a backlash. If your cat likes to ambush ankles or jump on shoulders, anticipate this and throw your cat a toy to play with instead.

Should your cat become aggressive for no obvious reason, he may be lashing out because he is in pain, so take him to the vet. Long-term aggression may result from your cat not having been socialized properly as a kitten. He may always remain wary of humans, but be patient and you may eventually gain his trust. In general, cats are much more docile after neutering.

Chewing and scratching

Boredom may lead to stress and destructive behavior. A cat that spends his life indoors, especially if he is often alone, may chew household objects to relieve the tedium. If this sounds like your cat, give him plenty of toys to play with and make sure you set aside some special time each day when you give him your full attention. Scratching is natural cat behavior that sharpens the claws and makes a visible and scented sign of a cat's territory. If your couch is becoming heavily scratched, buy a scratching post as an alternative for your cat to mark his territory. If he prefers to claw at the carpet, provide a horizontal scratching mat instead. Make sure that the material covering the post is different from that

CATS AT WAR

Aggression may occur between two previously friendly cats after an upset in their routines. For example, a cat that has spent some time away from home, such as at the vet, may be greeted with hostility on his return.

TERRITORIAL SIGN
Scratching tree bark is natural feline behavior. It leaves a visible and scented sign to other cats, warning them that they are now trespassing into another cat's area.

SCRATCHING POST
Your cat will continue his territorial behavior indoors (see left), so give him a dedicated scratching post to minimize damage to furniture.

of the couch. Place the post close to where your cat has been scratching. Rub some catnip into the post to tempt him if he is reluctant to use it. If he persists in scratching the furniture, deter him further by cleaning the scratched area to take away his scent—use rubbing alcohol, because cats hate the smell. Then cover the area in something that cats dislike the feel of, such as sticky, double-sided tape.

If he still will not stop, gently spray your cat's rump (never his head) with a water pistol whenever he scratches. You can also minimize damage from scratching by gluing small plastic caps over your cat's claws. These are available at pet stores but should only be used for permanently indoor cats.

Spraying

Like scratching, spraying marks territory, too, but this behavior usually disappears once a cat is neutered. It may recur if your cat becomes stressed by a change in his environment, such as the arrival of a baby or another pet.

To combat indoor spraying, distract your cat the moment you see him raise his tail to spray. Push his tail down or throw him a toy. If there is an area he sprays repeatedly, cleanse it thoroughly and place his food bowls there to deter further spraying. You can also line sprayed areas with aluminum foil, because cats dislike the sound of their urine hitting it.

Litter box problems

If your cat experiences pain when relieving himself, he may associate his discomfort with the litter box and go elsewhere. So when he relieves himself outside the box, seek a vet's advice. An all-clear from the vet will mean that the problem is probably something you are doing. If waste is not removed from the box frequently, your cat may find the box's odor overpowering. Similarly, adding a cover to the box to shield the smell from you may make the smell inside too much for him. Switching to a new type of litter can also cause problems, since your cat may find its texture unpleasant (p.211).

TOP TIPS

■ **To stop him from nibbling** on houseplants, coat the leaves in a strong-scented citrus spray that cats dislike.

■ **A pheromone treatment** from a vet can solve aggression or anxiety-related spraying.

■ **If you have two** indoor cats, give each a litter box. Some cats don't like sharing.

HEALTH AND BREEDING

HEALTH

Your greatest responsibility as an owner is your cat's health. You must ensure that your pet has regular checkups and vaccinations and be able to recognize any changes in his body or behavior that may require a trip to the vet. Educate yourself about common disorders and learn how to care for your cat when he is ill, recovering from surgery, or in an emergency.

Keep your cat free of itchy parasites

Finding and visiting a vet

Before bringing a cat home, look for a veterinary practice that will be willing to treat your cat. Your cat breeder may be able to recommend one. Alternatively, ask friends with cats or consult a local cat club or rescue center. Going to the vet is stressful for most cats, because they encounter strangers and other animals. Even a well-socialized cat will feel uneasy during the visit. Always take your cat in a carrier, with its door kept facing you in the waiting room so that he can see you. Speak to him soothingly and reward him with treats afterward.

If you buy a pedigree kitten, he should already have had his first vaccinations before you take him home at about 12 weeks old. Your breeder will give you the kitten's vaccination certificate, which you should show the vet on your initial visit. One of your earliest visits may be to have your cat neutered, generally from 4 months of age.

INITIAL VACCINATION
Cats should have their first vaccinations against infectious diseases, such as cat flu and feline leukemia, at between 9 and 12 weeks of age, followed by annual boosters for the rest of their lives.

EAR EXAMINATION
Your vet will examine the ears for mites during a routine checkup. Ear mites are highly contagious and commonly affect kittens and outdoor cats. They leave gritty debris in the ear canal that causes skin irritation.

Annual checkups

After his first visits, your cat will need a checkup annually, possibly twice a year in old age. The vet will assess his condition by checking his ears, eyes, teeth, gums, heartbeat, breathing, and weight, and feel him all over for abnormalities. A booster vaccination may be given. Your vet may clip your cat's claws if necessary, especially if he is a house cat or elderly. The vet will also inspect your cat for parasites and give you advice on administering worming and flea treatments.

THOROUGH EXAMINATION
During an annual checkup, the vet will examine your cat from head to tail, feeling for any tenderness or lumps. The vet will also listen to his heart and breathing to ensure there are no irregularities.

Common health problems

Every cat will experience health problems during his lifetime. Some complaints, such as a one-time incident of vomiting or diarrhea, are not a major cause for concern and do not require treatment by a vet. Other problems, such as intestinal worms or fleas, can be treated easily enough at home, following instructions from your vet. More serious disorders requiring urgent veterinary attention include: repeated vomiting or diarrhea—often a sign of an underlying disorder; urinary tract infections or obstructions, which can cause painful urination; eye problems, such as conjunctivitis or a visible third eyelid; abscesses from fights with other cats; and painful dental problems preventing your cat from eating.

CAT NOT EATING HIS FOOD
Refusing food is a cause for concern. It may indicate that your cat is in pain or has a serious illness needing urgent veterinary attention.

Signs of poor health

Cats tend to suffer in silence and do not draw attention to themselves when they are feeling vulnerable. One of your responsibilities as an owner is to be vigilant, keeping an eye out for any changes in your cat's routines and behavior that might suggest he needs veterinary attention.

Lethargy is difficult to spot—because cats generally rest much of the time—but decreased levels of activity, a reluctance to jump, and reduced alertness are often signs that your cat is ill or in pain. Lethargy is also often linked to obesity, so it may disappear when a cat loses his excess weight.

Changes in appetite are usually a sign of an underlying condition. A loss of appetite may be caused by pain in the mouth, such as toothache, or a more serious illness, such as kidney failure. Weight loss despite an increased appetite, together with increased urination and increased thirst, may be the result of an overactive thyroid or diabetes mellitus.

Abnormal or labored breathing may occur after a chest injury or as a result of an obstruction in the airway, an upper respiratory tract infection, or shock. Wheezing may be due to asthma or bronchitis. Breathing difficulties always require an emergency trip to the vet.

Dehydration is life-threatening and has various causes, including vomiting, diarrhea, increased urination, and heatstroke. You can carry out a simple test to check if your cat is dehydrated (see box, left). Emergency rehydration involves a vet injecting fluids under the skin or directly into a vein.

The color of a cat's gums (see box, left) can indicate several serious disorders, including those that affect the circulation of oxygen in the bloodstream. Lumps on skin, changes in grooming habits and coat texture, fur loss, and not using the litter box can also be signs of health problems.

TOP TIPS

■ **Dehydration test** Gently lift the skin up on the back of your cat's neck. If the skin springs back into position, your cat is healthy, but if it returns slowly, it is a sign of dehydration. Feel the gums with a finger—dry, tacky gums also indicate dehydration.

■ **Checking gums** A healthy cat has pink gums. Pale or white gums indicate shock, anemia, or blood loss; yellow gums are a sign of jaundice; red gums are caused by carbon-monoxide poisoning, fever, or bleeding in the mouth; blue gums suggest poor oxygenation of the blood.

First aid for cats

If your cat is injured, you may need to administer first aid before he has a chance to be seen by a vet. To treat a wound, apply pressure with a pad of clean cloth or gauze. Do not use tissue because it will stick to the wound. Keep the material in place, even if it becomes soaked with blood, until you see a vet. Removing an object embedded in a wound could cause more bleeding—leave it in place for your vet to treat.

A cat that has had an accident, such as being hit by a car, should be seen by a vet even if he has no visible injuries, since there could be internal bleeding, which can lead to shock.

TREATING SHOCK

A cat in shock may suffer from heat loss. Wrap him loosely in a blanket or quilt until he is assessed by a vet.

Shock is a life-threatening condition in which there is reduced blood flow, and tissues become starved of nutrients. Symptoms of shock include irregular breathing, anxiety, pale or blue gums, and a lowered body temperature. First aid for a cat in shock involves keeping him warm and elevating his hindquarters to increase blood flow to the brain while you take him to a vet.

If you find your cat unconscious, make sure his airway is not obstructed; listen and look for breathing; and feel for a pulse with a finger on one of the femoral arteries, which can be found on the inner side of his hindlegs, where they meet the groin. If there is no breathing, attempt artificial respiration by gently blowing air into your cat's lungs down the nostrils. If there is no heartbeat, alternate two breaths of artificial respiration with 30 chest compressions at two compressions per second.

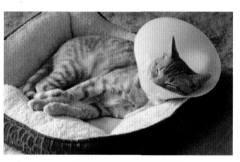

ELIZABETHAN COLLAR

After surgery, your cat may have to wear an Elizabethan collar for several days to prevent him from licking or chewing a wound that may have been stitched to help it repair.

BANDAGED LEG

A leg wound requires bandaging by a vet. Keep your cat inside if he has a bandaged limb. If the dressing becomes dirty, wet, loose, smelly, or uncomfortable, take your cat back to the vet for it to be changed.

When your cat is unwell

If your cat is ill or recovering from surgery or an accident, you must resist the temptation to stroke and cuddle him. He will most likely not enjoy being handled in the early stages of convalescence. Stroke or pet your cat only if he clearly wants attention. Provide him with a warm bed, where he can be left in peace to recuperate. Check on your cat regularly and change the bedding if it becomes soiled. If you have an outdoor cat, make sure he is kept indoors during his recovery and has easy access to bowls of water and a litter box.

Administering medicine

Only give your cat medicine prescribed by a vet, and follow the instructions carefully. You can try hiding a pill in a ball of meat or mold a sticky treat around it, but only if your cat is allowed to take food with his medicine. If not, or if he rejects or coughs up the pill, you will need to place it in his mouth (see below). This is best done with a helper to hold your cat while you insert the pill. If you are on your own, immobilize your cat by wrapping him in a towel, leaving his head exposed. Liquid medicines are also widely available and should be placed into the mouth, between the back teeth and cheek, using a plastic syringe without a needle

or a plastic medicine dropper. Drops for the eyes or ears can be administered while gently immobilizing your cat's head. Always make sure that the dropper does not touch his eyes or ears.

If your cat is wholly resistant to being given any kind of medicine at home, take him to your vet each day or have him kept at the practice until the course of treatment is over.

TOP TIPS

Caring for a convalescing cat:

■ Give frequent small portions of food heated to body temperature. You may have to hand-feed him initially.

■ Check your cat's wounds daily for redness or infection.

■ Provide a cozy bed, in a quiet location, with a microwavable heating pad or a hot-water bottle wrapped in a towel.

■ Keep other pets away from your cat while he is recuperating.

■ Give medicine according to your vet's instructions.

HEALTH | GIVING A PILL

1 Hold your cat's head with forefinger and thumb on either side of his mouth. Gently tilt his head back and pry open his jaws.

2 Place the pill as far back as possible on his tongue to trigger swallowing. Give him gentle encouragement while doing so.

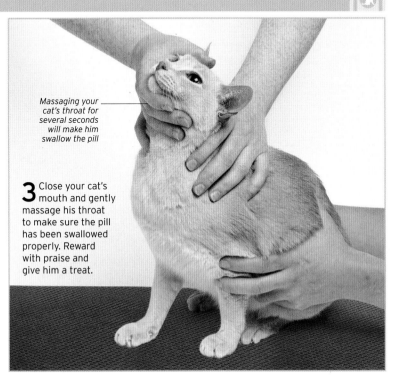

Massaging your cat's throat for several seconds will make him swallow the pill

3 Close your cat's mouth and gently massage his throat to make sure the pill has been swallowed properly. Reward with praise and give him a treat.

OVERWEIGHT CAT
If you cannot easily feel your cat's ribs or see a waist toward the back of his abdomen, he is overweight.

Weight problems

Various health problems are associated with obesity, including diabetes, cardiovascular disease, liver disease, and arthritis and mobility problems resulting from strain on joints. Weight gain may also make it difficult for your cat to groom himself.

If your cat is noticeably gaining weight, switch him to a low-calorie diet, provide fewer treats and meals, and increase his levels of exercise. Neutered cats are particularly at risk of weight gain, as are indoor cats, which may not exercise enough. Outdoor cats can put on weight if other people feed them, too. Cats usually live longer if they are a healthy weight.

Weight loss is also a cause for concern and should always be checked by a vet. It may be a sign of a serious disorder, such as an overactive thyroid gland.

Caring for an older cat

Most well-cared-for pet cats can live to the age of 14 or 15, with some occasionally reaching 20. The trend for cat life expectancy is climbing, with advances in disease prevention, a better understanding of diet, improved drugs and treatments, and more cats being kept indoors.

By about age 10, you may notice signs of aging in your cat: weight loss (or gain), deteriorating eyesight, dental disease, a decrease in mobility, less fastidious grooming, and a thinner, less shiny coat. His personality may change, too, with your cat becoming easily irritated and noisier, especially at night. As a senior, he may occasionally feel disoriented and relieve himself outside the litter box. You may want to start increasing his regular checkups by a vet to twice a year.

COMPARING LIFESPANS

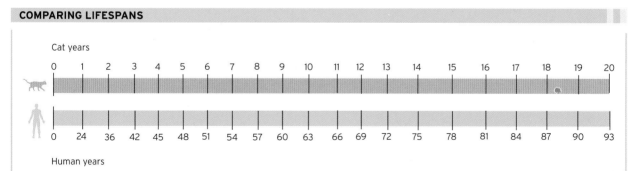

Cat years

| 0 | 1 | 2 | 3 | 4 | 5 | 6 | 7 | 8 | 9 | 10 | 11 | 12 | 13 | 14 | 15 | 16 | 17 | 18 | 19 | 20 |

| 0 | 24 | 36 | 42 | 45 | 48 | 51 | 54 | 57 | 60 | 63 | 66 | 69 | 72 | 75 | 78 | 81 | 84 | 87 | 90 | 93 |

Human years

It is often said that one year of a cat's life equates to seven years of a human's. But this does not hold, because life expectancy for pet cats has risen in recent years. It also ignores the different rates at which cats and humans develop: a 1-year-old cat can breed and raise kittens, which is a far more advanced stage than that of a 7-year-old child. By about 3, a cat is roughly equivalent to a person in their early 40s. Each cat year from then on corresponds to about three human years. Use the chart above to find an approximate human age for your cat.

INHERITED DISORDERS

Some diseases and disorders are passed down from one generation of cats to the next. Different cat breeds have their own inherited health problems, usually as a result of inbreeding among a relatively small population. Responsible breeders should not breed from cats known to have faulty genes, and screening tests for many of these disorders are now available.

Cats with flat faces may suffer from breathing difficulties

Breed-specific problems

Because the gene pool may be quite small for each cat breed, faulty genes can have a greater influence than they would in a larger mixed-cat population, where such genes usually vanish after a few generations. Some cat breeds are even characterized by inherited disorders—for example, in the past, the crossed eyes of classic Siamese cats were the result of a visual problem. An inherited disorder may be present when a kitten is born or develop later in a cat's life. Some cats may have a faulty gene but never develop any symptoms. These cats are called carriers and can produce kittens with the inherited disease if they breed with another cat carrying the same faulty gene.

Many cat diseases are thought to be genetic in origin but have not yet had faulty genes identified to explain them. The disorders in the table below have all been confirmed as genetic. For some of them, screening tests are available to identify whether or not a cat has the faulty gene. To help eradicate inherited disorders, responsible breeders should avoid using any cats known to have or to carry an inherited disorder for breeding by having them neutered.

If your cat has or develops an inherited disorder, try to find out as much information as possible about the condition. Most inherited disorders are not curable, but careful management can reduce symptoms and allow a good quality of life for your pet.

DISEASE	DESCRIPTION	CAN SCREENING DETECT IT?	MANAGING THE DISEASE	BREEDS OF CAT AFFECTED
Primary seborrhea	Flaky or greasy skin and hair.	No specific screening test available.	Wash the affected cat frequently with medicated shampoo.	Persian, Exotic
Congenital hypotrichosis	Kittens are born with no hair and are susceptible to infection.	No test currently available for this rare disorder.	No treatment. Keep the cat in a warm indoor environment, away from potential sources of infection.	Birman
Bleeding disorders	Excessive or abnormal bleeding after injury or trauma.	Yes. There are tests available for some types of bleeding disorder.	Look for nonhealing wounds on your cat. Try to staunch blood flow and seek veterinary advice.	Birman, British Shorthair, Devon Rex
Pyruvate kinase deficiency	A condition that affects life span and the number of red blood cells, leading to anemia.	Yes. A genetic test is available.	Affected cats may need blood transfusions.	Abyssinian, Somali

DISEASE	DESCRIPTION	CAN SCREENING DETECT IT?	MANAGING THE DISEASE	BREEDS OF CAT AFFECTED
Glycogenosis	Inability to metabolize glucose properly, leading to severe muscle weakness then heart failure.	Yes. A genetic test is available.	No treatment. Affected cats will need short-term fluid therapy.	Norwegian Forest Cat
Hypertrophic cardiomyopathy	Thickening of the heart muscle, usually results in heart failure.	Yes. A genetic test is available.	Drugs may be given to minimize the effects of heart failure.	Maine Coon, Ragdoll
Spinal muscular atrophy	Progressive muscular weakness, beginning in the hind limbs. Appears in kittens from 15 weeks old.	Yes. A genetic test is available.	No treatment. In some cases, an affected cat may survive with an adequate quality of life if given support.	Maine Coon
Devon Rex myopathy	General muscle weakness, an abnormal gait, and problems with swallowing.	No. Disorder first appears in kittens at 3-4 weeks old.	No treatment. Give affected cats small, liquid meals to avoid risk of choking.	Devon Rex
Hypokalemic polymyopathy	Muscle weakness, associated with kidney failure. Affected cats often have a stiff gait and head tremors.	Yes. A genetic test is available for Burmese cats.	The condition can be managed with oral potassium.	Burmese, Asian Leopard
Lysosomal storage disease	Any of various enzyme deficiencies that affect many body systems, including the nervous system.	Yes. Some types of the disease can be screened and tested for.	No effective treatment. Affected cats usually die young.	Persian, Exotic, Siamese, Oriental, Balinese, Burmese, Asian Leopard, Korat
Polycystic kidney disease	Pockets of fluid (cysts) develop in the kidneys, eventually causing kidney failure.	Yes. A genetic test is available.	No cure. Drugs can be given to ease the workload of the kidneys.	British Shorthair, Persian, Exotic
Progressive retinal atrophy	Degeneration of the rods and cones in the retina of the eyes, leading to early blindness.	Yes. There is a test available for one form of the disorder, found in Abyssinians and Somalis.	No cure. Affected cats should be kept as safe as possible, away from potential hazards.	Abyssinian, Somali, Persian, Exotic
Osteochondrodysplasia	Painful degenerative joint disorder, leading to the fusion of tail, ankle, and knee bones.	No. To help prevent the disorder, cats with folded ears should only be crossed with cats with normal ears.	Palliative treatment can help ease pain and swelling of joints.	Scottish Fold
Manx syndrome	A condition where the spine is too short, leading to spinal-cord damage and affecting the bladder, bowels, and digestion.	No. There is no specific test for this severe form of taillessness.	No treatment. Most kittens are euthanized when the disease becomes apparent.	Manx

RESPONSIBLE BREEDING

A litter often includes a
mixture of coat colors

Breeding purebred cats may sound like an enjoyable—and potentially lucrative—endeavor, but becoming a breeder is a big commitment. Most successful breeders have years of experience behind them. If you decide to go ahead, be ready to put lots of time (and money) into research, preparation, and caring for your pregnant cat and her newborn kittens.

A big decision

Before trying your hand as a breeder, make sure you know what you are getting yourself into. Get as much advice and detailed information as possible. The breeder from whom you bought your purebred female cat will be able to give you valuable tips, including where to find a suitable purebred tom to father the kittens. You will need a thorough understanding of cat genetics, especially coat colors and patterns, because the litter may have a mix of characteristics. You must also be aware of genetic diseases associated with your breed (pp.244-245). Purebred kittens sell for hundreds of dollars, but most of this income will be offset by costs for the stud fee, veterinary fees, heating for the kittens, registration fees, and extra food for the mother and kittens (once they are weaned). There may also be the long-term cost of owning more cats if you can't find suitable homes for your kittens.

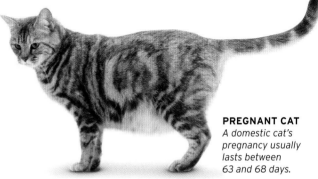

PREGNANT CAT
A domestic cat's pregnancy usually lasts between 63 and 68 days.

Pregnancy and birth

If the mating was successful, your cat will be visibly pregnant by about four weeks. Give her extra food and ask your vet about any supplements she might need. Toward the end of her pregnancy, make a nest for her out of a cardboard box containing plain paper that she can tear up. You will need to be around for the birth to ensure it runs smoothly. Make sure you know what to expect—your vet can advise you about what will happen at each stage of the birth. After that, your main job will be to socialize the kittens so they'll be ready for new homes when they are about 12 weeks old.

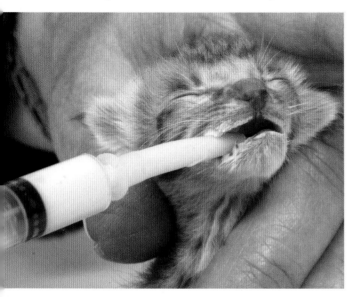

HAND FEEDING
If a kitten is not thriving, you will need to feed him a cat-milk substitute from a pipette, about every two hours. Ask your vet about how to do this.

NEUTERING

Surgical sterilization, or neutering, is advised for any cat you don't intend to breed. In males, the testes are removed in a simple operation. Neutered males rarely spray indoors. They are less aggressive and less likely to get injured in territorial battles or catch diseases from fighting or mating. Neutering females, called spaying, is major surgery in which the ovaries and part of the uterus are removed. It has a positive effect on longevity, eliminating the risk of common cancers in female cats.

HAPPY FAMILY
If all the kittens are healthy, the only assistance the mother will need will be extra food to help her produce milk for her litter. If she trusts you, she may let you handle her kittens from the start.

GLOSSARY

Albinism: Lack of the pigment that gives color to skin, hair, and eyes. In cats, true albinism is very rare, but partial albinism gives rise to pointed coat patterns, as in the Siamese, and color variations, such as silver tabby.

Allele: Variant form of a gene. Cats have two alleles of each gene—one inherited from each parent.

Almond-shaped eyes: Oval eyes with flattened corners, seen in breeds such as the Abyssinian and Siamese.

Awn hairs: Slightly longer bristly hairs that, together with the soft down hairs, constitute the undercoat.

Bicolor: Coat pattern combining white with another color.

Blotched tabby: Alternative term for Classic Tabby.

Blue: Light- to medium-gray coat color, a diluted form of black. Blue-only cat breeds include the Russian Blue, Korat, and Chartreux.

Bracelets: Dark horizontal bands on the legs of a tabby cat.

Break: *see* Stop

Breeches: In longhaired cats, extra-long hair on the upper back part of the hindlegs.

Breed standard: Detailed description produced by a cat registry that defines the required standards for a pedigree cat's conformation, coat, and color.

Calico: Tortie and white patterning.

Cameo: Red, or its diluted form cream, where white covers two-thirds of the hair shaft.

Carnivore: Meat-eating animal.

Cat fancier: Enthusiast for breeding and showing purebred cats.

Cat registry: Organization that sets breed standards and registers the pedigrees of cats.

CFA: The Cat Fanciers' Association, the world's largest registry of pedigree cats, based in the US.

Chocolate: Pale- to medium-brown coat color.

Chromosome: Threadlike structure within a cell nucleus containing genes arranged along a strand of DNA. Cats have 38 chromosomes arranged in 19 corresponding pairs. (Humans have 46, arranged in 23 pairs.)

Classic tabby: *see* Tabby

Cobby: Compact, muscular, heavy-boned body type, seen in breeds such as the Persian.

Colorpoint: *see* Pointed

Crossbreed: *see* Random-bred

Curled ears: Ears that curve backward, as in the American Curl.

Diluted/dilution: Paler version of a color caused when the dilution gene comprises two recessive alleles—for example, black becomes blue and red becomes cream.

Domestic cat: Any member of *Felis catus*, pedigree or mixed breed. Also commonly known as a house cat.

Dominant: Describes an allele inherited from one parent that overrides the effect of a paired recessive allele inherited from the other parent. For example, the allele for a tabby coat is dominant.

Double coat: Fur consisting of a thick, soft undercoat covered by a protective topcoat of longer guard hairs.

Down: Short, soft, fine hairs that form an undercoat in some breeds.

Feathering: Longer hair on areas such as legs, feet, and tail.

Feral: Describing a domesticated species that has reverted to a wild state.

FIFe: Fédération Internationale Féline, the leading European federation of cat registries.

Folded ears: Ears that fold forward and down, seen in breeds such as the Scottish Fold.

GCCF: The Governing Council of the Cat Fancy, the leading organization for the registration of cats in the UK.

Gene pool: The complete collection of genes within an interbreeding population.

Ghost markings: Faint tabby markings on the coat of a solid-colored cat that show up in certain lights.

Ground color: Background color in tabbies. There are many variants: brown, red, and silver are among the most common.

Guard hairs: Longer, tapering hairs that form a cat's topcoat and provide weatherproofing.

Hybrid: Offspring of two different species—for example, the Bengal, which is a cross between the domestic cat (*Felis catus*) and the Asian leopard (*Felis bengalensis*).

Leather: Hairless area at the end of the nose. Color varies according to coat color and is defined in the breed standards for pedigree cats.

Lilac: Warm pink-gray color, a diluted form of brown.

"M" mark: Typical "M"-shaped mark on the forehead of tabby cats; also known as a frown mark.

Mackerel tabby: *see* Tabby

Marbled: Variation of the Classic Tabby, mostly seen in wildcat hybrids such as the Bengal.

Mascara lines: Dark lines running from the outer corners of the eyes or encircling the eyes.

Mask: Dark coloration on the face, usually around the muzzle and eyes.

Mitted: Color pattern in which the paws are white. Also called mittens or socks.

Moggie: Informal term for a non-pedigree cat.

Mutation: Change in a cell's DNA, often arising by chance; effects of genetic mutations in cats include hairlessness, folded or curled ears, curly coats, and short tails.

Particolor: General term for a coat pattern that has two or more colors, often one being white.

Patched tabby: Tortoiseshell with tabby markings.

Pedigree: Purebred.

Pointed: Coat pattern in which a cat has pale body fur with darker extremities (head, tail, and legs); typically seen in the Siamese.

Polydactyly: Extra toes produced by a genetic mutation; polydactyly, or polydactylism, is common in certain breeds, but only in the Pixiebob is the trait accepted in the breed standard.

Random-bred: Cat of mixed parentage.

Recessive: An allele that can produce an effect only when inherited from both parents. If a recessive allele from one parent is paired with a dominant allele from the other parent, its effect will be overridden. The alleles for certain eye colors and long fur in cats are recessive.

Red: Reddish-brown, used to describe certain coat colors in Abyssinian and Somali cats; known as sorrel in the UK.

Rex coat: Curly or wavy coat, as seen in Devon and Cornish Rex cats.

Roan: Coat with an evenly distributed mixture of colored and white hairs.

Ruddy: A color of Abyssinian cats; known as usual in the UK.

Ruff: Frill of longer hair around the neck and chest.

Selective breeding: Mating of animals that possess desired traits, such as a particular coat color or pattern.

Semi-longhair: Medium-long coat, usually with a minimal undercoat.

Sepia: Dark-brown ticking on a paler ground color.

Shaded: Coat pattern in which the final quarter of each hair is colored.

Single coat: Coat with just one layer, usually the topcoat of guard hairs, seen in such cats as the Balinese and Turkish Angora.

Smoke: Coat pattern in which each hair shaft is pale at the base and colored for about half of its length.

Solid: Coat in which a single color is distributed evenly along the hair shaft; known as self in the UK.

Spotted tabby: see Tabby

Stop: Indentation between the muzzle and the top of the head; also known as a break.

Tabby: Genetically dominant coat pattern that comes in four types: Classic Tabby has a blotched or whorled pattern; Mackerel Tabby has fishbone stripes; Spotted Tabby has spots or rosettes; Ticked Tabbies have a faint pattern on a ticked coat.

Temperament: The character of a cat.

TICA: The International Cat Association, a genetic registry for pedigree cats worldwide.

Ticked: Coat pattern in which each hair shaft has alternate bands of pale and darker colors; also known as agouti. See also Tabby.

Tipped: Coat pattern in which just the tip of each hair is strongly colored.

Topcoat: Outer coat of guard hairs.

Tortie: Common abbreviation for tortoiseshell.

Tortoiseshell: Coat pattern in which black and red hairs, or their diluted forms, are mixed in patches.

Tricolor: Term sometimes used to describe a coat of two colors plus white.

Tufts: Clusters of longer hairs that are seen, for example, between the toes or on the ears.

Undercoat: Layer of hair beneath the topcoat, usually short and often woolly.

Van pattern: Pointed coat pattern in which the color is restricted to the ears and tail only, as in the Turkish Van.

Wedge: Triangular facial conformation seen in most cats except the flat-faced Persian; the shape is elongated in breeds such as the Siamese and Orientals.

Whippy: Of a tail, thin and elastic.

Whisker pads: Fleshy pads on either side of a cat's muzzle where the whiskers are placed in rows.

Wirehair: Rare coat type caused by a genetic mutation in which the hairs are twisted or bent at the tips, giving a coarse, springy texture; seen in the American Wirehair cat.

INDEX

INDEX continued

INDEX continued

ACKNOWLEDGMENTS

Dorling Kindersley would like to thank the following people for their help in the preparation of this book: For allowing us to photograph their cats: Sphynx and Devon Rex–Susan Rust (ketcherex.tripod.com); Selkirk Rex, Scottish Fold, and British Shorthair–Jan Bradley (www.sheephouse.co.uk); Maine Coon and Ragdoll–Dorothea Uebele (www.applause-pedigreecats.co.uk); Pixiebob and Bengal–Joolz Scarlett(www.arcatia-bengals.com); Siamese and Oriental Shorthair–Pat Cherry (www.ciatra-siamese-orientals.co.uk); Bengal–E. A. Slater (www.junglefirebengals.co.uk); Persian–Isobella Bangs (lafrebella.tripod.com); American Curl and British Shorthair–Claire Winman (www.americancurls.com).

Tadley Pet Supplies, Baughurst, Hampshire (www.tadleypetsupplies.co.uk), for the loan of cat toys and equipment; Paul Self for equipment photography; Rob Nunn for additional picture research; Mitun Banerjee for design help; Alison Logan for advice on the "Health and Breeding" chapter; Caroline Hunt for proofreading; and Helen Peters for the index;DK India would like to thank Nityanand Kumar for high-res assistance, and Priyanka Sharma and Saloni Singh for jackets assistance.

The publisher would like to thank the following for their permission to reproduce their photographs: (Key: a-above; b-below/bottom; c-center; f-far; l-left; r-right; t-top)

5 Animal Photography: Tetsu Yamazaki (bl). **6-7 Getty Images:** Michelle McMahon/Flickr Open. **9 Alamy Images:** Blickwinkel (br). **Dreamstime.com:** Natalya Sidorova (tr). **10 Dreamstime.com:** Dragonika (cl). **11 Dreamstime.com:** Lrlucik. **12 Dreamstime.com:** Melinda Fawver (bl). **13 Dreamstime.com:** Pjatochka (cl). **14 fotoLibra :** Darran Scott (b). **20 Alamy Images:** Juniors Bildarchiv GmbH (bl). **21 Dreamstime.com:** Marko Bojanovic. **22 Alamy Images:** Juniors Bildarchiv GmbH (b). **23 Alamy Images:** ZUMA Press, Inc. (bl). Dreamstime.com: Jura Vikulin (tr). **24-25 Alamy Images:** Juniors Bildarchiv GmbH. **27 Animal Photography:** Sally Anne Thompson (bl). **28 Shutterstock.com:** Eric Isselee (cla). **29 Alamy Images:** Petographer (ca). Janet Poulsen:

(b, tr). **31 Larry Johnson:** (cl, b, tr). **37 Dreamstime.com:** Sheila Bottoms. **40 Ardea:** Jean-Michel Labat (cl, tr); Jean Michel Labat (b). **41 Alamy Images:** Tierfotoagentur (cl, tr, b). **46 Animal Photography:** Alan Robinson (cl, tr, b). **51 Animal Photography:** Helmi Flick (cl, tr, b). **52 Kevin Workman:** (tr). **53 Alamy Images:** Juniors Bildarchiv GmbH (cl, b, tr). **54-55 Dorling Kindersley:** Tracy Morgan- Animal photography. **58 Chanan Photography:** (cl, b, tr). **59 Animal Photography:** Alan Robinson (cl, tr). **61 Animal Photography:** Tetsu Yamazaki (b). **Dreamstime.com:** Vladyslav Starozhylov (cl, tr). **62-63 Alamy Images:** Zoonar GmbH. **65 Fotolia:** Callalloo Candcy. **67 Corbis:** Yoshihisa Fujita/MottoPet/amanaimages. **68-69 Dorling Kindersley:** Tracy Morgan-Animal Photography. **72-73 Dreamstime.com:** Lilun. **75 Shutterstock.com:** Nynke van Holten (cla). **78 Alamy Images:** Juniors Bildarchiv GmbH (cl); Tierfotoagentur (tr, b). **79 Animal Photography:** Tetsu Yamazaki (cl, tr, b). **80 Shutterstock.com:** Vivienstock (cra). **81 Alamy Images:** MJ Photography (b). **82 Petra Mueller:** (cl, bl, br, tr). **84-85 Animal Photography:** Alan Robinson. **86 Animal Photography:** Helmi Flick (cl, tr, b). **87 SuperStock:** Marka (b, cl, c, tr). **88 Getty Images:** Datacraft Co Ltd. **90 Chanan Photography:** (cl, tr). Robert Fox: (b). **91 Animal Photography:** Helmi Flick (cl, tr, c, b). **93 Animal Photography:** Tetsu Yamazaki (cl, tr, b). **Dreamstime.com:** Sarahthexton (c). **96 Alamy Images:** Juniors Bildarchiv GmbH (c, tr, b). **naturepl.com:** Ulrike Schanz (cl). **97 Animal Photography:** Helmi Flick (tr); Tetsu Yamazaki (cl, b). **98 Animal Photography:** Helmi Flick (b, tr). **SuperStock:** Juniors (cl). **99 Animal Photography:** Helmi Flick (b). **Ardea:** Jean-Michel Labat (cl, tr). **100 Getty Images:** Benjamin Torode/Flickr. **101 Dreamstime.com:** Ekaterina Cherkashina (cl, b); Linncurrie (c, tr). **102 Animal Photography:** Helmi Flick (cl, b, tr). **103 Alamy Images:** Idamini (c, tr, b). **104 Animal Photography:** Helmi Flick (c, tr, b). **105 Animal Photography:** Helmi Flick (cl, tr, b). **106-107 Dorling Kindersley:** Tracy Morgan-Animal Photography. **108 Animal Photography:** Helmi Flick (cl, tr, b). **109 Animal Photography:** Tetsu Yamazaki (cl, tr, b). **110 Alamy**

Images: Juniors Bildarchiv GmbH (c). **Animal Photography:** Alan Robinson (cl). **111 Animal Photography:** Helmi Flick (cl, tr, b). **112 Dreamstime.com:** Elena Platonova (tr, b); Nelli Shuyskaya (cl). **113 Animal Photography:** Helmi Flick (cl, b, tr). **114 Animal Photography:** Sally Anne Thompson. **116 Chanan Photography:** (tr, cl, b). **117 Dave Woodward:** (cl, b, tr). **118 Robert Pickett** / www.robertpickett.com. **119 Dorling Kindersley:** Tracy Morgan-Animal Photography. **120 Animal Photography:** Artem Furman (cl, tr, b). **121 Fotolia:** eSchmidt (cl, tr, b). **122 Alamy Images:** Tierfotoagentur (cl, tr, b). **123 Animal Photography:** Alan Robinson (cl, tr, b). **FLPA:** S. Schwerdtfeger / Tierfotoagentur (b, tr). **124-125 Dorling Kindersley:** Tracy Morgan-Animal Photography. **126 Dreamstime.com:** Oleg Kozlov. **128-129 Dorling Kindersley:** Tracy Morgan-Animal Photography. **130 Alamy Images:** Juniors Bildarchiv GmbH (tr, b); Tierfotoagentur (cl). **131 Animal Photography:** Tetsu Yamazaki (cl, tr, b). **132 Dorling Kindersley:** Dawn Trick (cl). **135 Dreamstime.com:** Victoria Purdie (bl). **136-137 Dorling Kindersley:** Tracy Morgan-Animal Photography. **138 Chanan Photography:** (b, tr, c). **143 Alamy Images:** Juni.rs Bildarchiv GmbH. **Dreamstime.com:** Petr Jilek (cl, tr). **144-145 Alamy Images:** JTB Media Creation, Inc.. **147 Chanan Photography:** (b, cl, tr). **148 Dreamstime.com:** Isselee (cl, tr, b). **151 Chanan Photography:** (b, tr, cl). **153 Alamy Images:** Petra Wegner. **158 Chanan Photography:** (tr, cl, b). **163 Alamy Images:** PhotoAlto. **164-165 Dorling Kindersley:** Tracy Morgan-Animal Photography. **166-167 Corbis:** Julie Habel. **168 Science Photo Library:** Mark Taylor / Nature Picture Library (cla).**169 Animal Photography:** Tetsu Yamazaki (cl, b, tr). **171 Alamy Images:** Petra Wegner (cl, tr, b). **172 Animal Photography:** Tetsu Yamazaki (cl, tr, b). **173 Dreamstime.com:** Prillfoto (tr). **174-175 Alamy Images:** Juniors Bildarchiv GmbH. **174 Ardea:** Jean-Michel Labat (b). **177 Alamy Images:** Tierfotoagentur (cl, bl, tr). **Animal Photography:** Tetsu Yamazaki (cl, tr, b). **179 Animal Photography:** Tetsu Yamazaki (cl, tr, b). **180 Animal Photography:** Tetsu Yamazaki (cl, b, tr). **181 Animal Photography:** Tetsu Yamazaki (cl, tr, b). **182 Animal Photography:** Helmi

Flick (c, tr, b). **184-185 Dorling Kindersley:** Tracy Morgan-Animal Photography. **186 Alamy Images:** Idamini (tl, tr, b). **187 Alamy Images:** Idamini. **188 Chanan Photography:** (cl, tr, b). **189 Animal Photography:** Helmi Flick (cl, tr, b). **190-191 Dorling Kindersley:** Tracy Morgan-Animal Photography. **193 Animal Photography:** Helmi Flick (tr, b); Tetsu Yamazaki (cl). **194 Animal Photography:** Tetsu Yamazaki (cl, tr, b). **195 Olga Ivanova:** (cl, tr, b). **196 Animal Photography:** Helmi Flick (cl, tr, b). **197 Animal Photography:** Leanne Graham. **198 Alamy Images:** Corbis Premium RF (bl). **199 Dreamstime.com:** Ijansempoi. **200-201 Alamy Images:** Arco Images GmbH. **202 Dreamstime.com:** Joyce Vincent (bl). **203 Alamy Images:** imagebroker (cl). **Corbis:** Michael Kern/Visuals Unlimited (tc). **204 Dreamstime.com:** Stuart Key (tr). **205 Alamy Stock Photo:** Juniors Bildarchiv GmbH (tc). Dr. Catsby®: (tr). **207 Corbis:** Image Source (tr). **Dreamstime.com:** Maxym022 (br). **210 Alamy Images:** Juniors Bildarchiv GmbH (l). **212 Photoshot:** NHPA (b). **214 Dreamstime.com:** Miraswonderland (t). **215 Alamy Images:** Juniors Bildarchiv GmbH (tr). **216 Dreamstime.com:** Frenc (tr); Eastwest Imaging (l). **217 Alamy Images:** Juniors Bildarchiv GmbH (bl). **218 Dreamstime.com:** Jeroen Van Den Broek (cr). **219 Dreamstime.com:** Niderlander (br). **220 Corbis:** Frank Lukasseck (b). **221 Dreamstime.com:** Mitja Mladkovic. **223 Dreamstime.com. 224 Dreamstime.com:** Mimnr1 (tr). **Fotolia:** Callalloo Candcy. **225 Alamy Images:** Rodger Tamblyn (crb). **226 Dreamstime.com:** Miradrozdowski (cr). **231 Alamy Images:** Juniors Bildarchiv GmbH (cl, tr). **232 Ardea:** John Daniels (bl). **233 Dreamstime.com:** Willeecole (r). **235 Dreamstime.com:** Jana Horová (l). **236-237 Corbis:** D. Sheldon/F1 Online. **238 Fotolia:** Eléonore H (cr). **239 Getty Images:** Fuse. **240 Alamy Stock Photo:** Juniors Bildarchiv GmbH (m). **241 Getty Images:** Danielle Donders–Mothership Photography/Flickr Open (cb). **243 Fotolia:** svetlankahappy (tl). **247 Photoshot:** Juniors Tierbildarchiv

All other images © Dorling Kindersley. For further information see: www.dkimages.com